CW00347788

'No peas for the wicked'

KipperWilliams

VISTA

Thanks are due to the following where some cartoons originally appeared:
Guardian Finance & European business pages; *Radio Times*; *Sunday Times* book section;
Private Eye; *Spectator*; *Time Out*

First published in Great Britain 1996
as a Vista paperback original

Vista is an imprint of the Cassell Group
Wellington House, 125 Strand, London WC2R 0BB

© Kipper Williams 1996

The right of Kipper Williams to be identified as author of this work has been asserted by him in accordance with the Copyright,
Designs and Patents Act, 1988.

A catalogue record for this book is available from the British Library

ISBN 0 575 60099 3

Layout by Fishtail Design

Printed and bound in Great Britain by
Hillman Printers Ltd

All rights reserved. No part of this publication may be reproduced or transmitted in any form or by any means, electronic or mechanical including
photocopying, recording or any information storage or retrieval system, without prior permission in writing from the publishers.
This book is sold subject to the condition that it shall not, by way of trade or otherwise, be lent, resold, hired out, or otherwise circulated without the
publisher's prior consent in any form of binding or cover other than that in which it is published and without a similar condition including this condition
being imposed on the subsequent purchaser.

96 97 98 99   10 9 8 7 6 5 4 3 2 1

For Pamela, Callum and Dylan

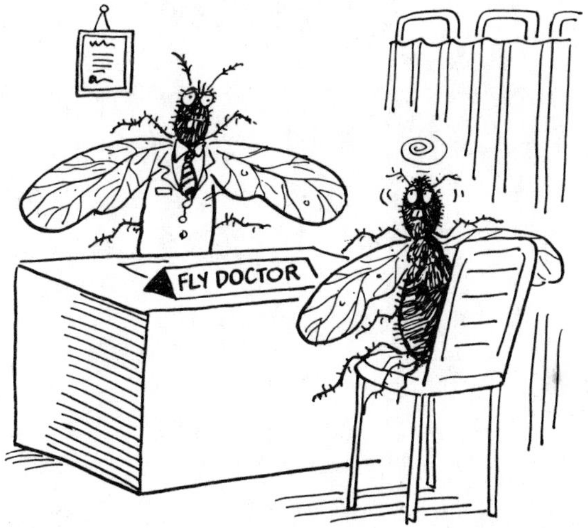
FLY DOCTOR

"You should try and take things easier, Mr. Blue Arse."

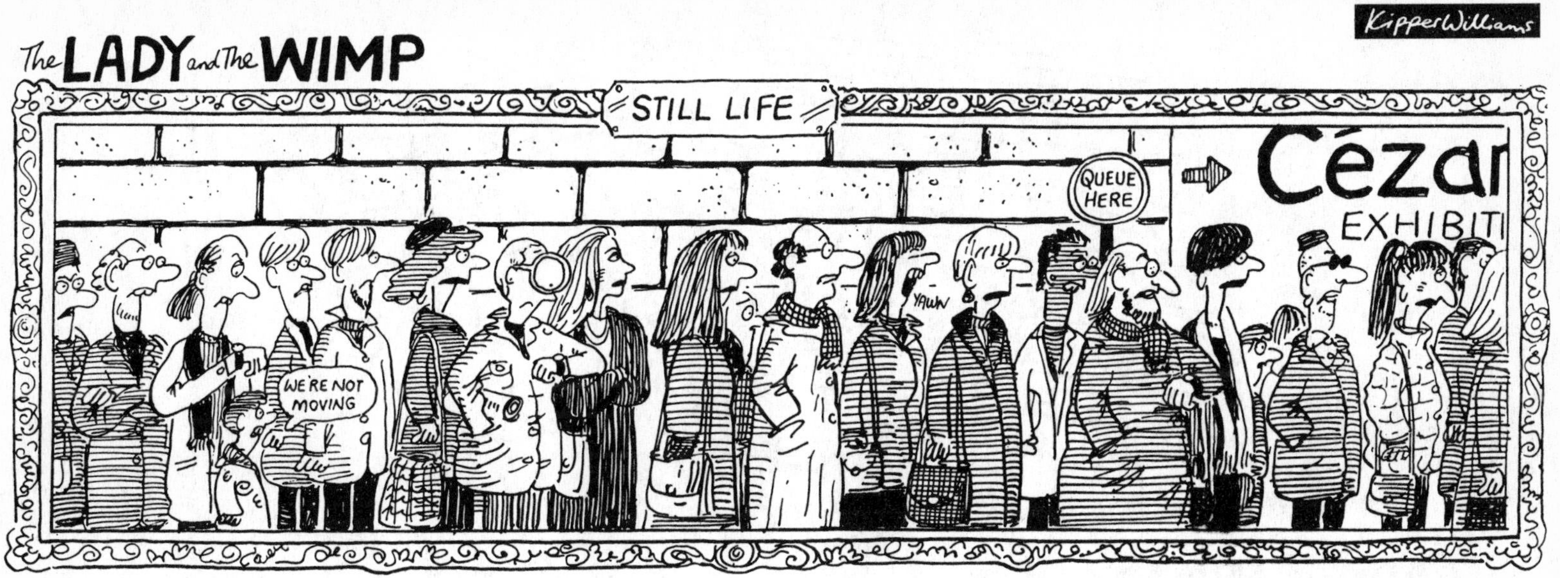
KipperWilliams
The LADY and The WIMP
STILL LIFE
QUEUE HERE
→ Cézar
EXHIBITI
WE'RE NOT MOVING
YAWN

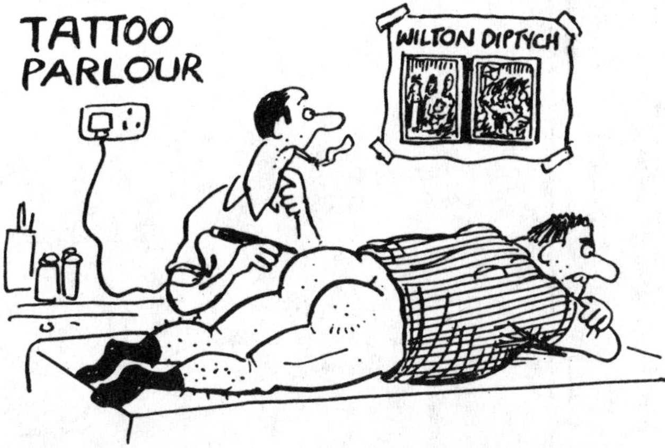
TATTOO PARLOUR
WILTON DIPTYCH

Kipper Williams

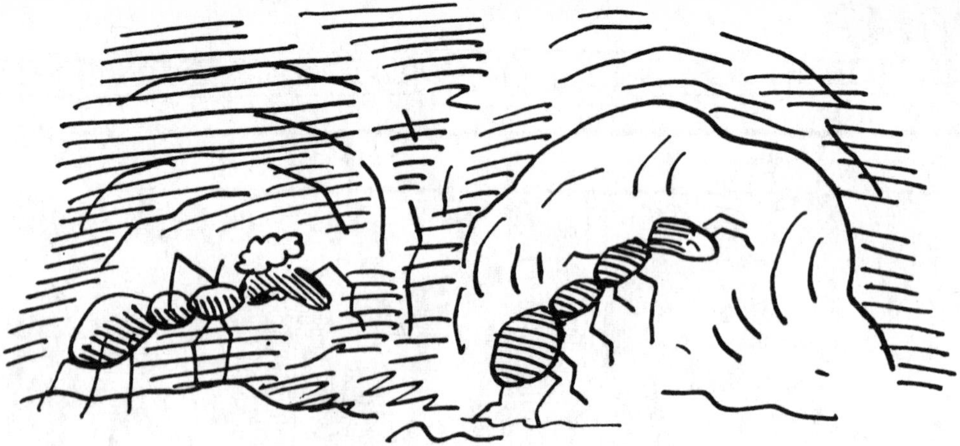

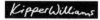

'Work – that's all you think about.'

The LADY and The WIMP

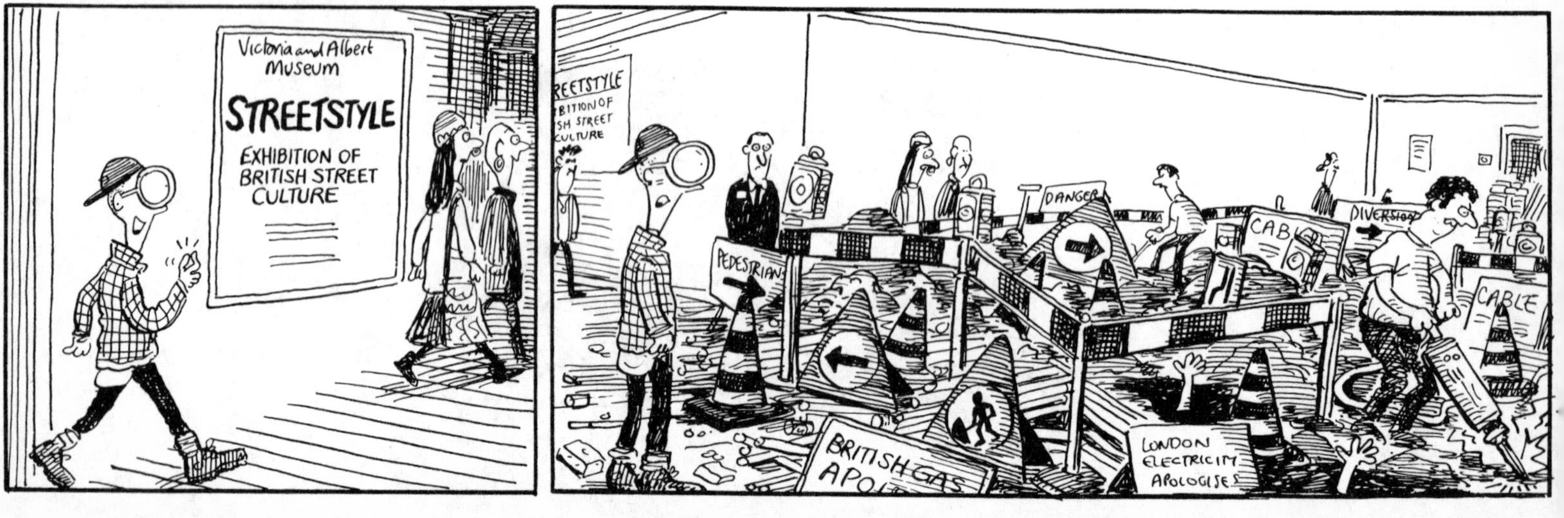
Victoria and Albert Museum
STREETSTYLE
EXHIBITION OF BRITISH STREET CULTURE
PEDESTRIANS
DANGER
DIVERSION
CABLE
LONDON ELECTRICITY APOLOGISES

The LADY and The WIMP

Kipper Williams

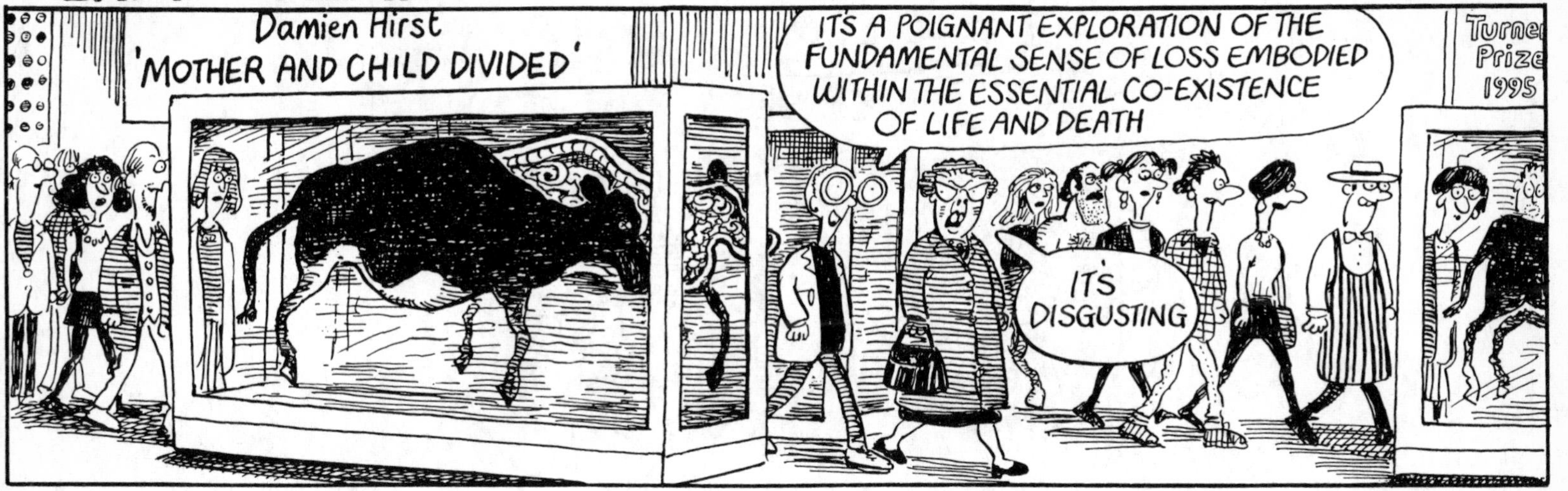
Damien Hirst
'MOTHER AND CHILD DIVIDED'
ITS A POIGNANT EXPLORATION OF THE FUNDAMENTAL SENSE OF LOSS EMBODIED WITHIN THE ESSENTIAL CO-EXISTENCE OF LIFE AND DEATH
Turner Prize 1995
IT'S DISGUSTING

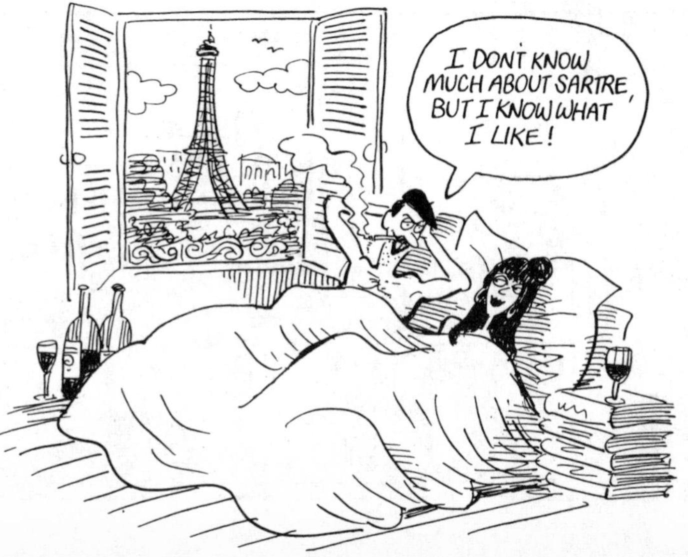
I DON'T KNOW MUCH ABOUT SARTRE, BUT I KNOW WHAT I LIKE!

Kipper Williams

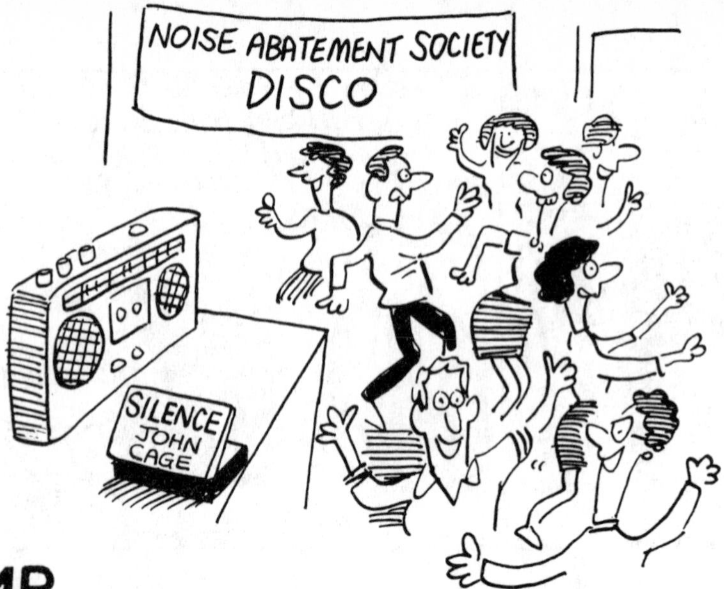
NOISE ABATEMENT SOCIETY
DISCO
SILENCE
JOHN CAGE

The LADY and The WIMP

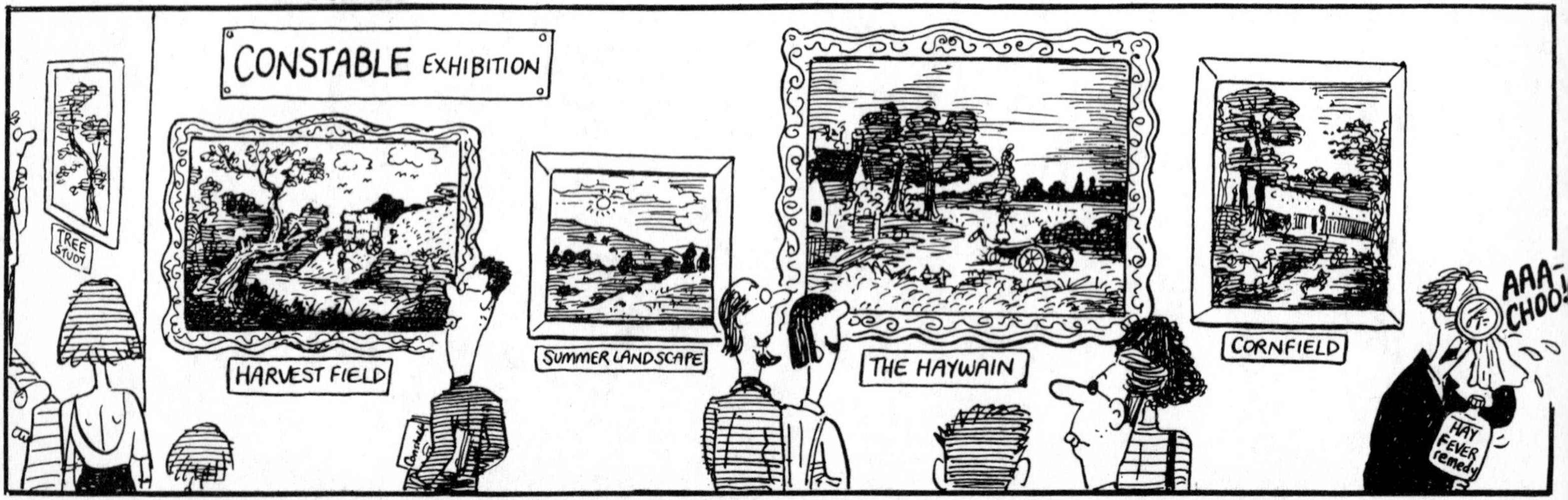
CONSTABLE EXHIBITION
TREE STUDY
HARVEST FIELD
SUMMER LANDSCAPE
THE HAYWAIN
CORNFIELD
AAA-CHOO!
HAY FEVER remedy

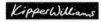

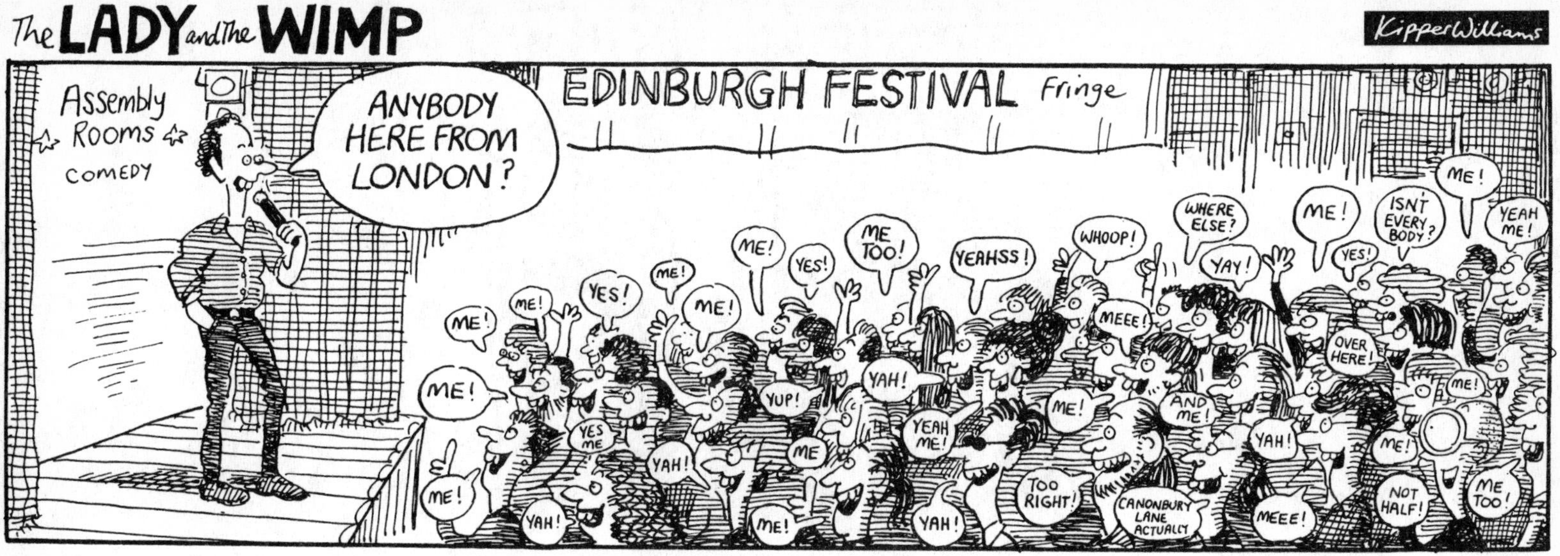
The LADY and the WIMP
Kipper Williams
Assembly Rooms
COMEDY
EDINBURGH FESTIVAL Fringe
ANYBODY HERE FROM LONDON?
ME!
ME!
YES!
ME!
ME!
ME!
YES!
ME TOO!
YEAHSS!
WHOOP!
WHERE ELSE?
YAY!
ME!
YES!
ISN'T EVERY BODY?
ME!
YEAH ME!
MEEE!
OVER HERE!
ME!
YUP!
YAH!
ME!
AND ME!
ME!
YES ME
YAH!
ME
YEAH ME!
YAH!
ME!
ME!
TOO RIGHT!
CANONBURY LANE ACTUALLY
MEEE!
NOT HALF!
ME TOO!
YAH!
ME!
YAH!

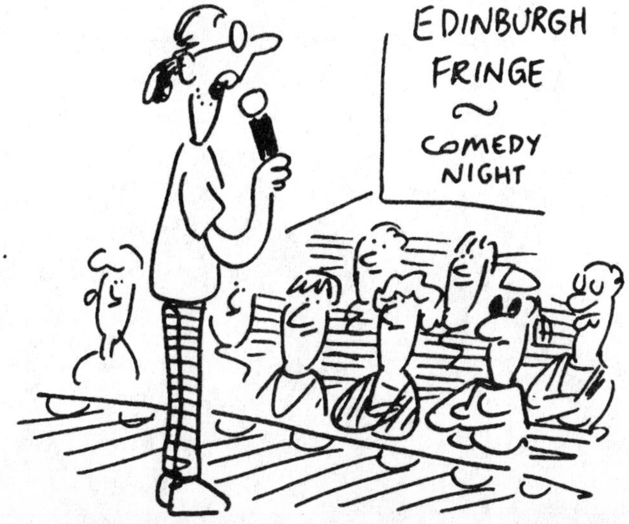
EDINBURGH FRINGE
~
COMEDY NIGHT

'Take my partner – I wish you would!'

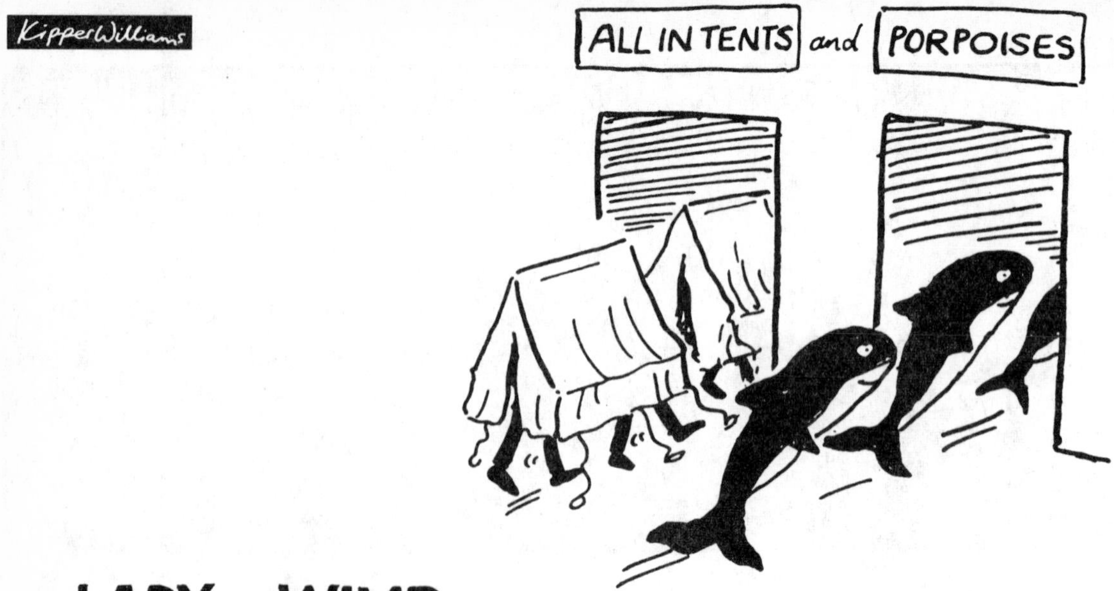
KipperWilliams
ALL IN TENTS and PORPOISES

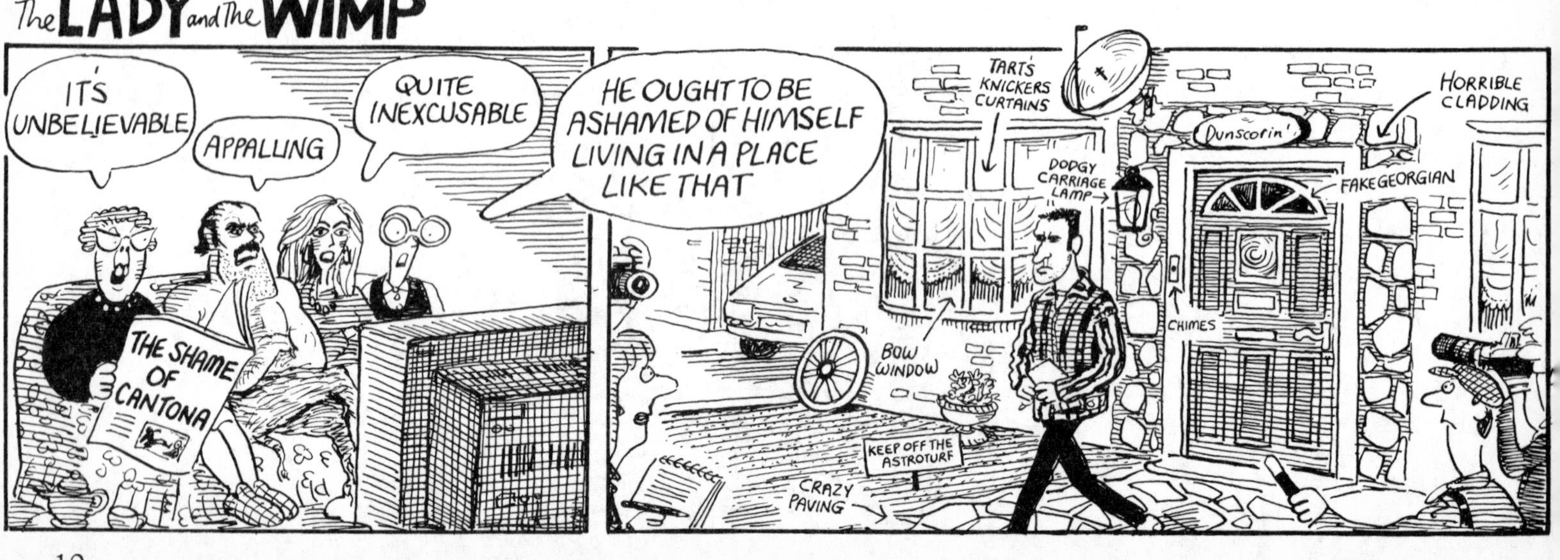
The LADY and The WIMP
IT'S UNBELIEVABLE
APPALLING
QUITE INEXCUSABLE
HE OUGHT TO BE ASHAMED OF HIMSELF LIVING IN A PLACE LIKE THAT
THE SHAME OF CANTONA
TARTS KNICKERS CURTAINS
HORRIBLE CLADDING
Dunscorin'
DODGY CARRIAGE LAMP
FAKE GEORGIAN
CHIMES
BOW WINDOW
KEEP OFF THE ASTROTURF
CRAZY PAVING

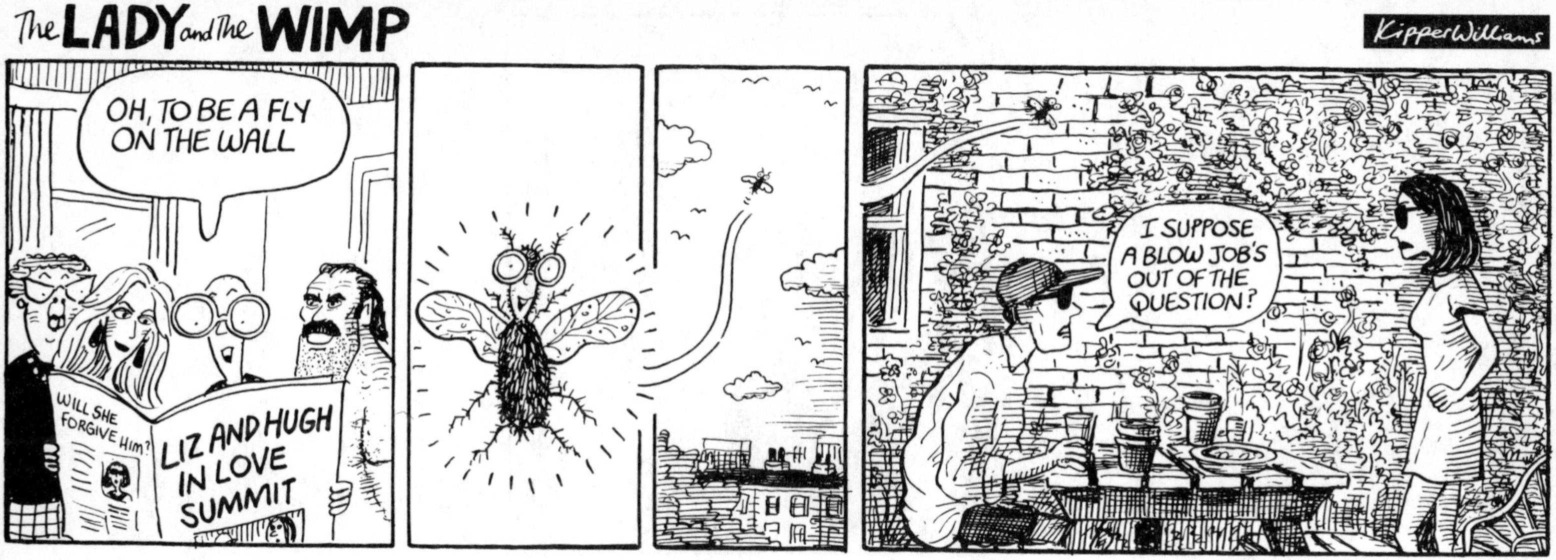
The LADY and The WIMP
Kipper Williams
OH, TO BE A FLY ON THE WALL
WILL SHE FORGIVE HIM?
LIZ AND HUGH IN LOVE SUMMIT
I SUPPOSE A BLOW JOB'S OUT OF THE QUESTION?

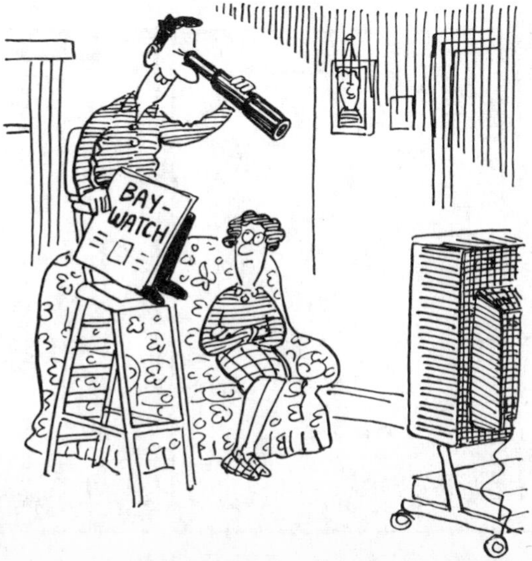
BAY-WATCH

Kipper Williams

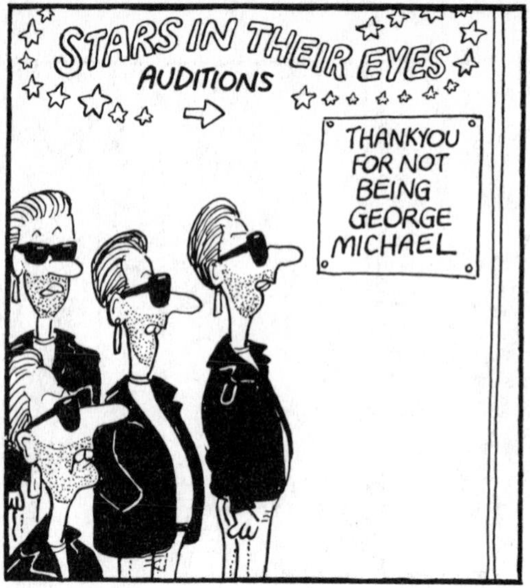
STARS IN THEIR EYES
AUDITIONS
THANKYOU FOR NOT BEING GEORGE MICHAEL

The LADY and The WIMP

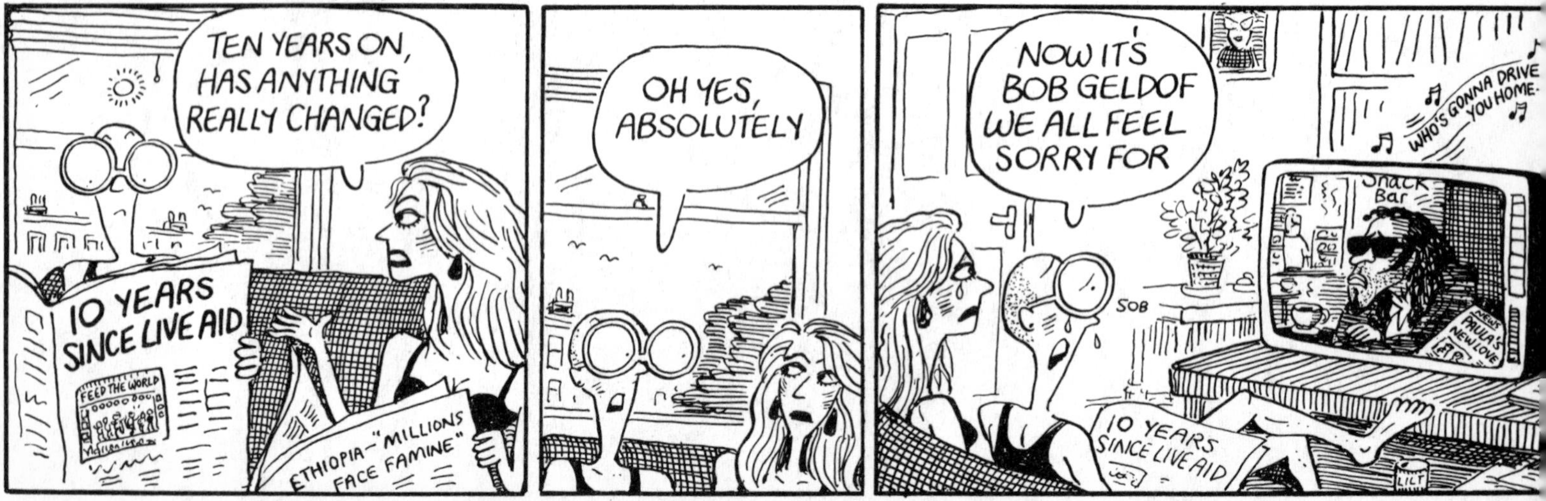
TEN YEARS ON, HAS ANYTHING REALLY CHANGED?
10 YEARS SINCE LIVE AID
FEED THE WORLD
ETHIOPIA–"MILLIONS FACE FAMINE"
OH YES, ABSOLUTELY
NOW IT'S BOB GELDOF WE ALL FEEL SORRY FOR
WHO'S GONNA DRIVE YOU HOME.
Snack Bar
SOB
NEWS PAULA'S NEW LOVE
10 YEARS SINCE LIVE AID
LILT

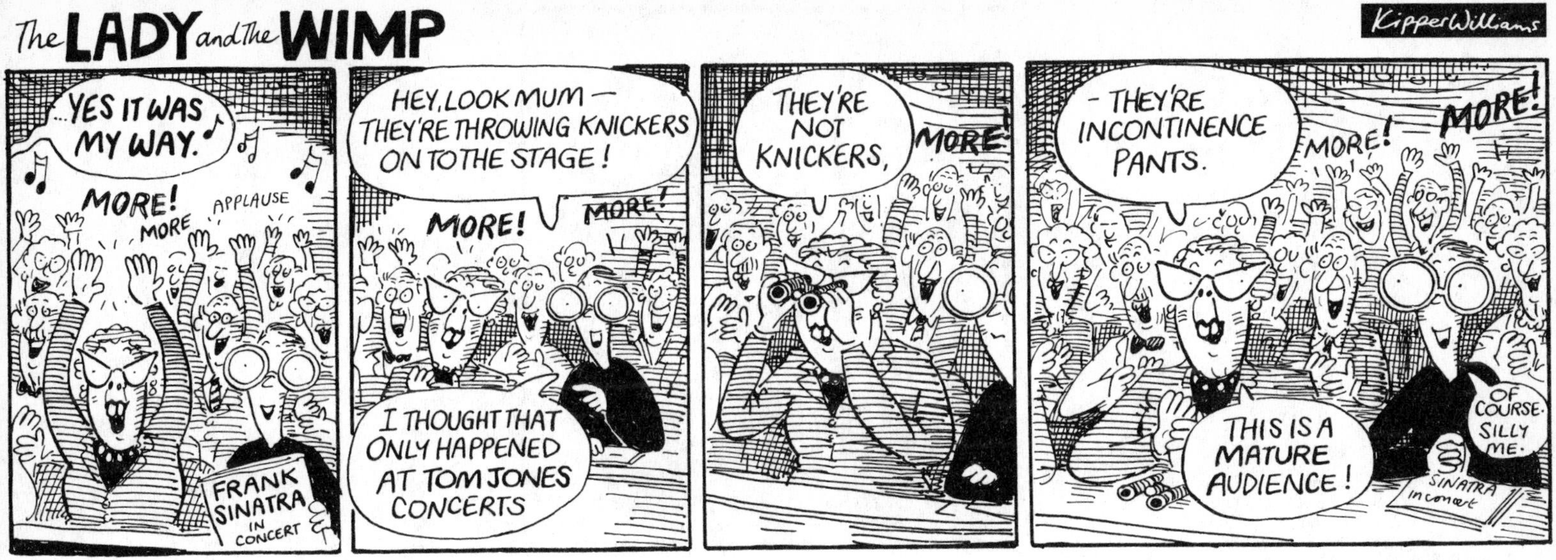
The LADY and The WIMP
Kipper Williams
...YES IT WAS MY WAY.
MORE!
MORE
APPLAUSE
FRANK SINATRA IN CONCERT
HEY, LOOK MUM — THEY'RE THROWING KNICKERS ON TO THE STAGE!
MORE!
MORE!
I THOUGHT THAT ONLY HAPPENED AT TOM JONES CONCERTS
THEY'RE NOT KNICKERS,
MORE!
- THEY'RE INCONTINENCE PANTS.
MORE!
MORE!
THIS IS A MATURE AUDIENCE!
OF COURSE. SILLY ME.
SINATRA in concert

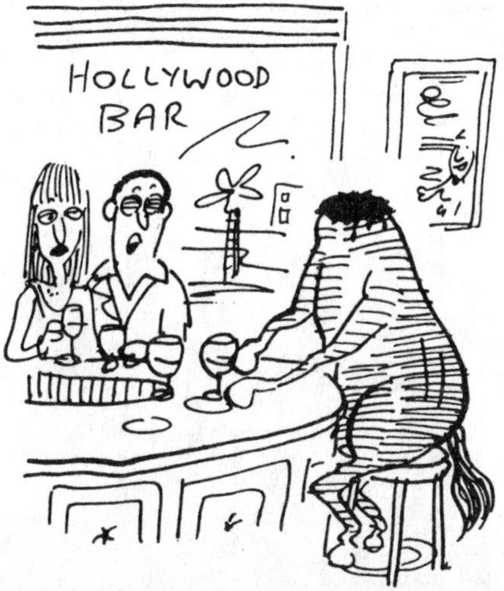
HOLLYWOOD BAR

'He hasn't worked since The Godfather!'

Kipper Williams

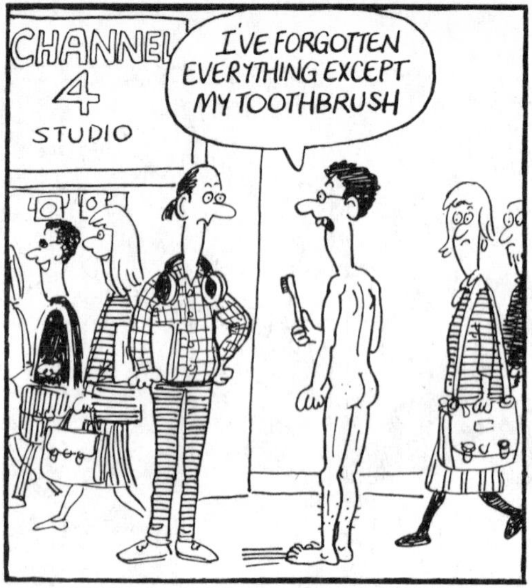
CHANNEL 4 STUDIO
I'VE FORGOTTEN EVERYTHING EXCEPT MY TOOTHBRUSH

The LADY and The WIMP

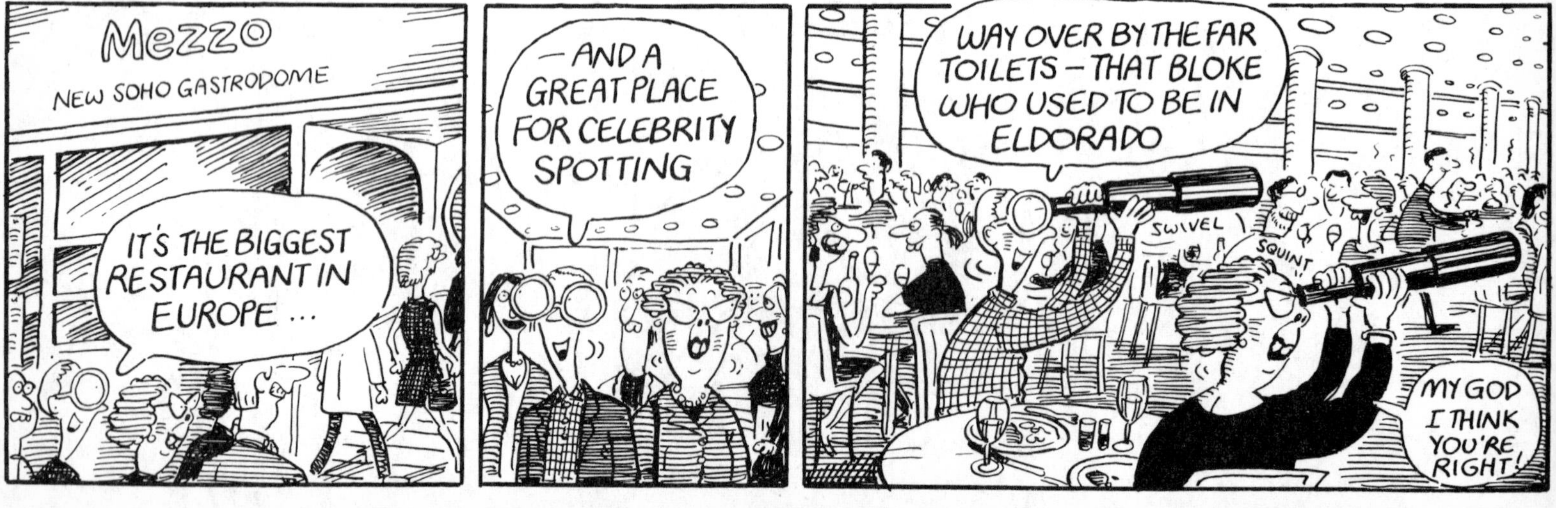
Mezzo
NEW SOHO GASTRODOME
IT'S THE BIGGEST RESTAURANT IN EUROPE ...
— AND A GREAT PLACE FOR CELEBRITY SPOTTING
WAY OVER BY THE FAR TOILETS — THAT BLOKE WHO USED TO BE IN ELDORADO
SWIVEL
SQUINT
MY GOD I THINK YOU'RE RIGHT!

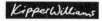

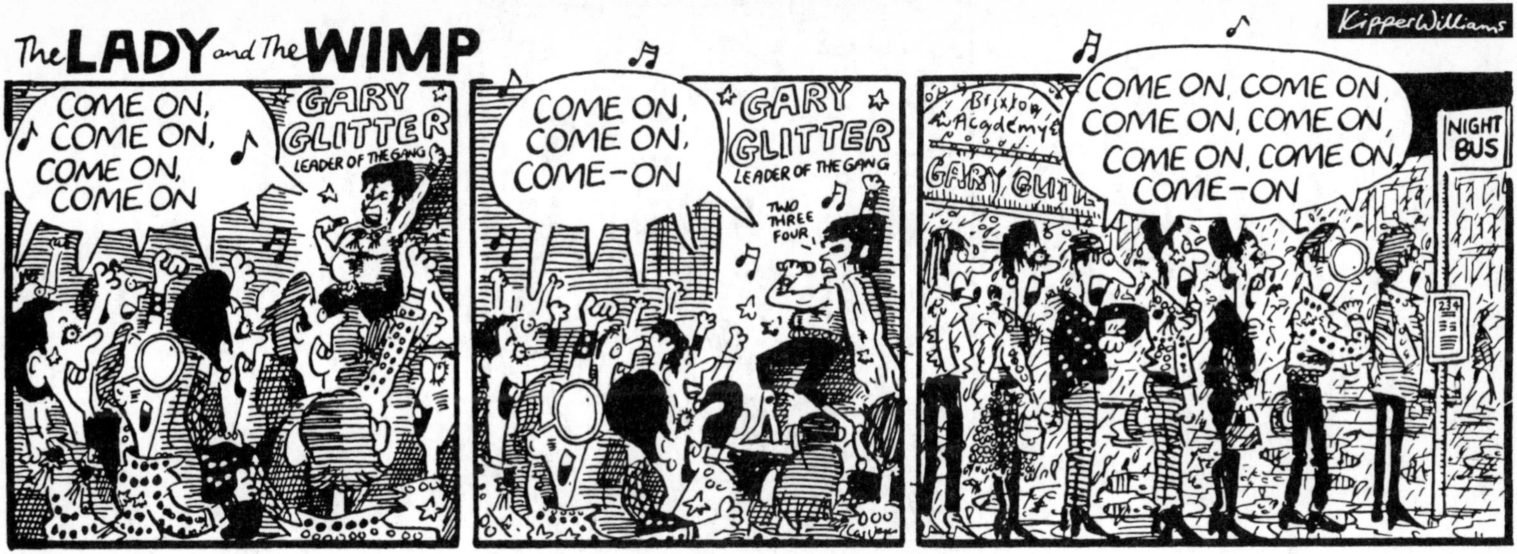
The LADY and The WIMP
Kipper Williams
COME ON, COME ON, COME ON, COME ON
GARY GLITTER
LEADER OF THE GANG
COME ON, COME ON, COME-ON
GARY GLITTER
LEADER OF THE GANG
TWO THREE FOUR
Brixton Academy
GARY GLITT
COME ON, COME ON, COME ON, COME ON, COME ON, COME ON, COME-ON
NIGHT BUS
234

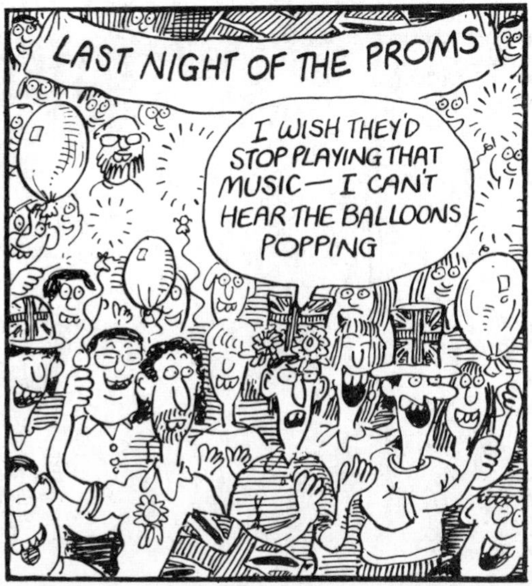
LAST NIGHT OF THE PROMS
I WISH THEY'D STOP PLAYING THAT MUSIC— I CAN'T HEAR THE BALLOONS POPPING

Kipper Williams

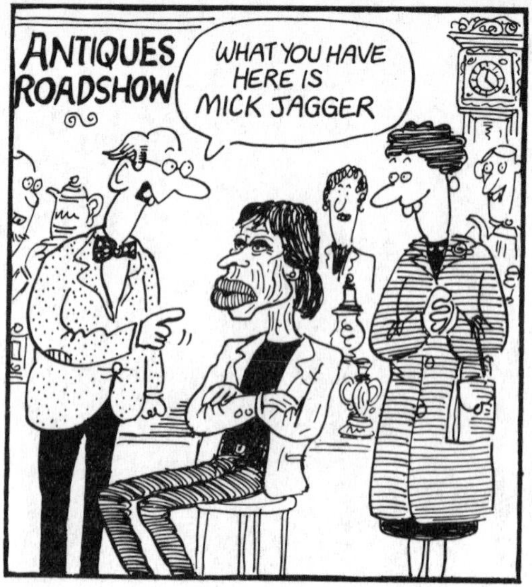
ANTIQUES ROADSHOW
WHAT YOU HAVE HERE IS MICK JAGGER

The LADY and the WIMP

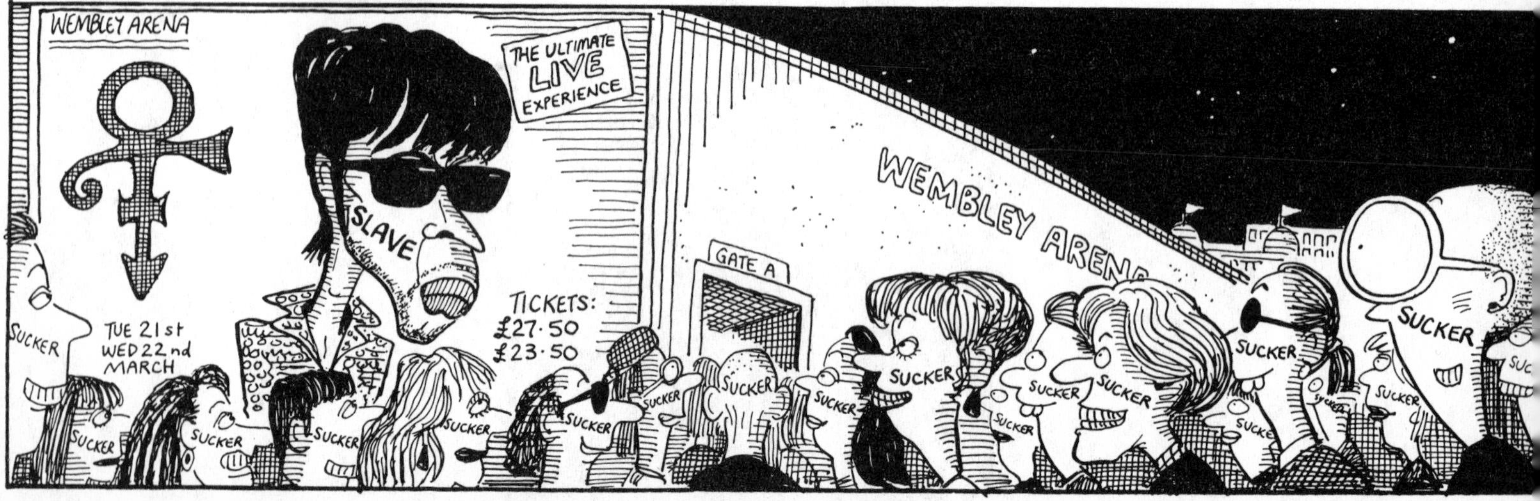
WEMBLEY ARENA
THE ULTIMATE LIVE EXPERIENCE
SLAVE
TUE 21st WED 22nd MARCH
TICKETS: £27·50 £23·50
WEMBLEY ARENA
GATE A
SUCKER

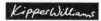

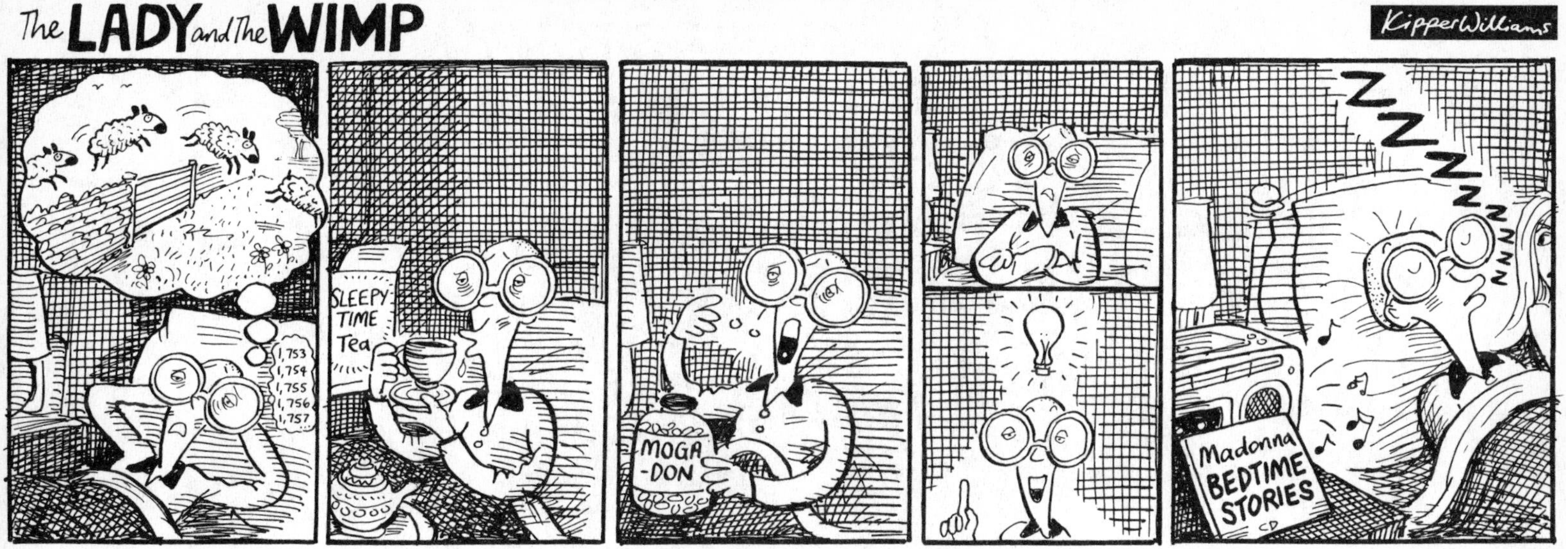
The LADY and The WIMP
Kipper Williams
1,753
1,754
1,755
1,756
1,757
SLEEPY TIME Tea
MOGA -DON
Madonna
BEDTIME STORIES
CD

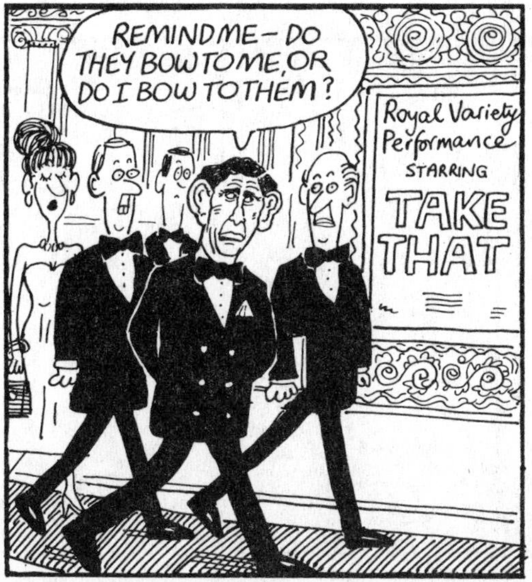
REMIND ME – DO THEY BOW TO ME, OR DO I BOW TO THEM?
Royal Variety Performance
STARRING
TAKE THAT

Kipper Williams

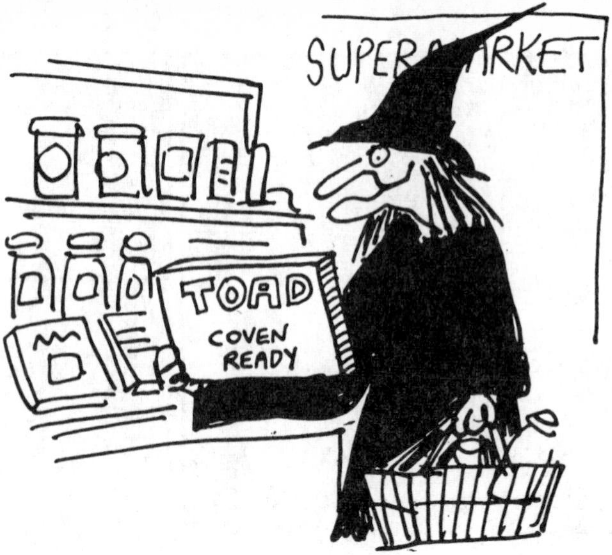
SUPERMARKET
TOAD
COVEN READY

The LADY and The WIMP

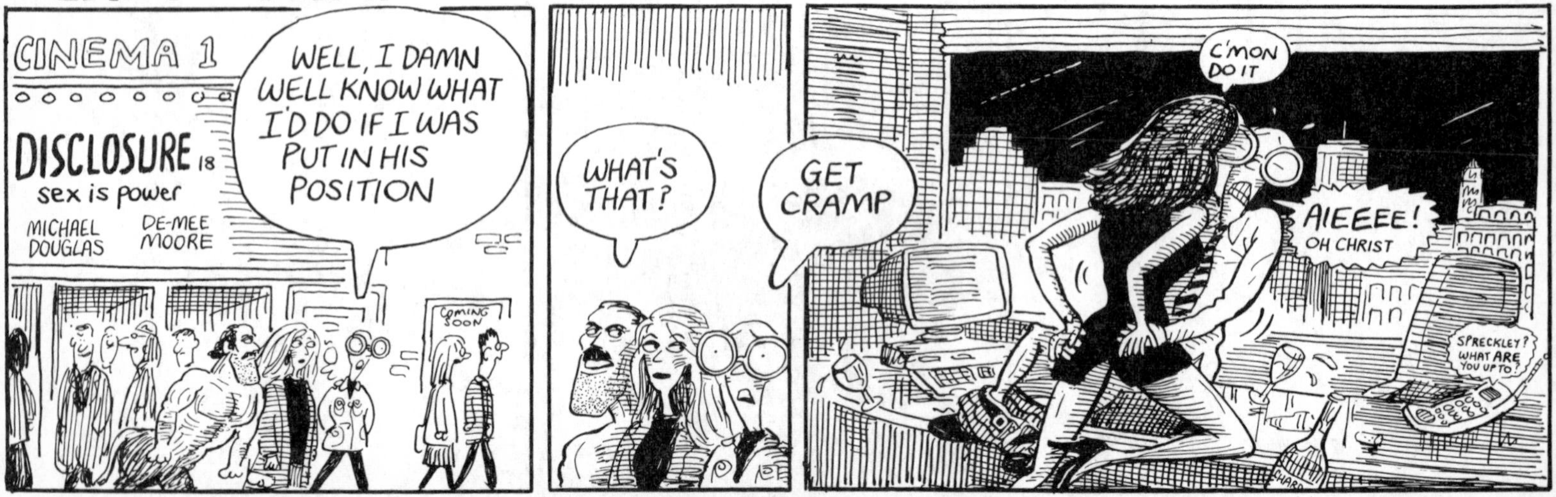
CINEMA 1
DISCLOSURE 18
sex is power
MICHAEL DOUGLAS
DE-MEE MOORE
COMING SOON
WELL, I DAMN WELL KNOW WHAT I'D DO IF I WAS PUT IN HIS POSITION
WHAT'S THAT?
GET CRAMP
C'MON DO IT
AIEEEE! OH CHRIST
SPRECKLEY? WHAT ARE YOU UP TO?

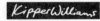

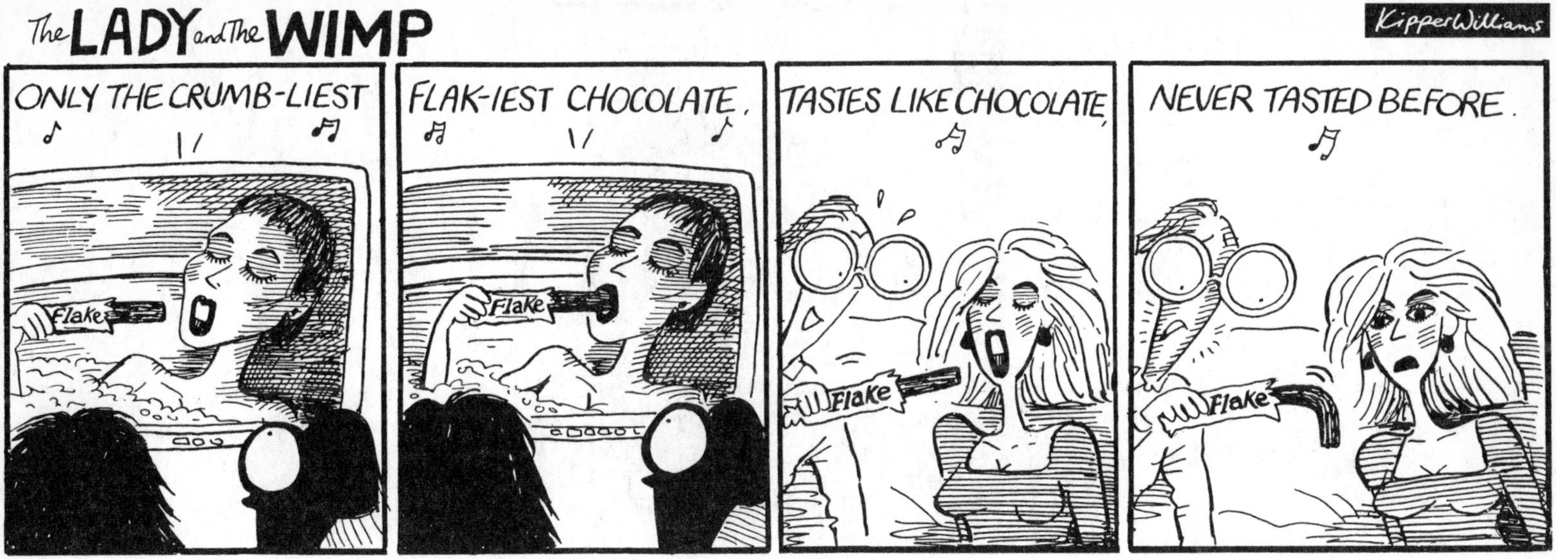
The LADY and The WIMP
Kipper Williams
ONLY THE CRUMB-LIEST
Flake
FLAK-IEST CHOCOLATE,
Flake
TASTES LIKE CHOCOLATE,
Flake
NEVER TASTED BEFORE.
Flake

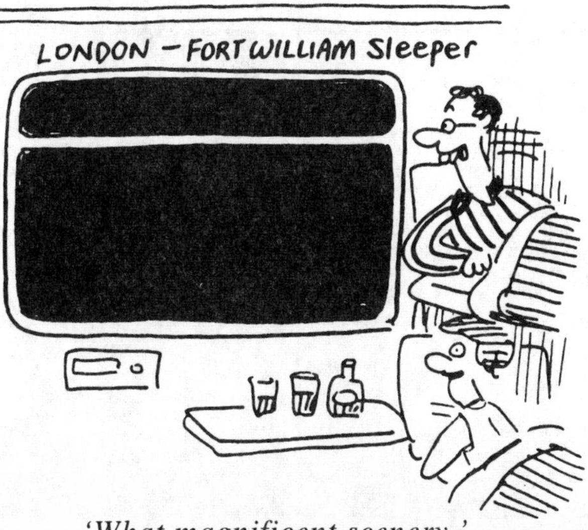
LONDON – FORT WILLIAM Sleeper

'What magnificent scenery.'

Kipper Williams

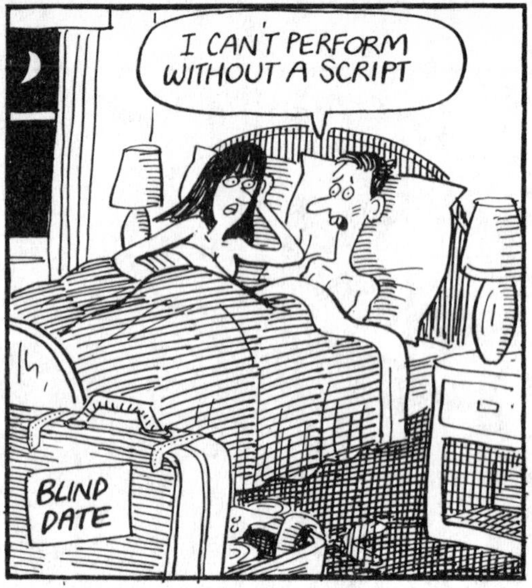
I CAN'T PERFORM WITHOUT A SCRIPT
BLIND DATE

The LADY and The WIMP

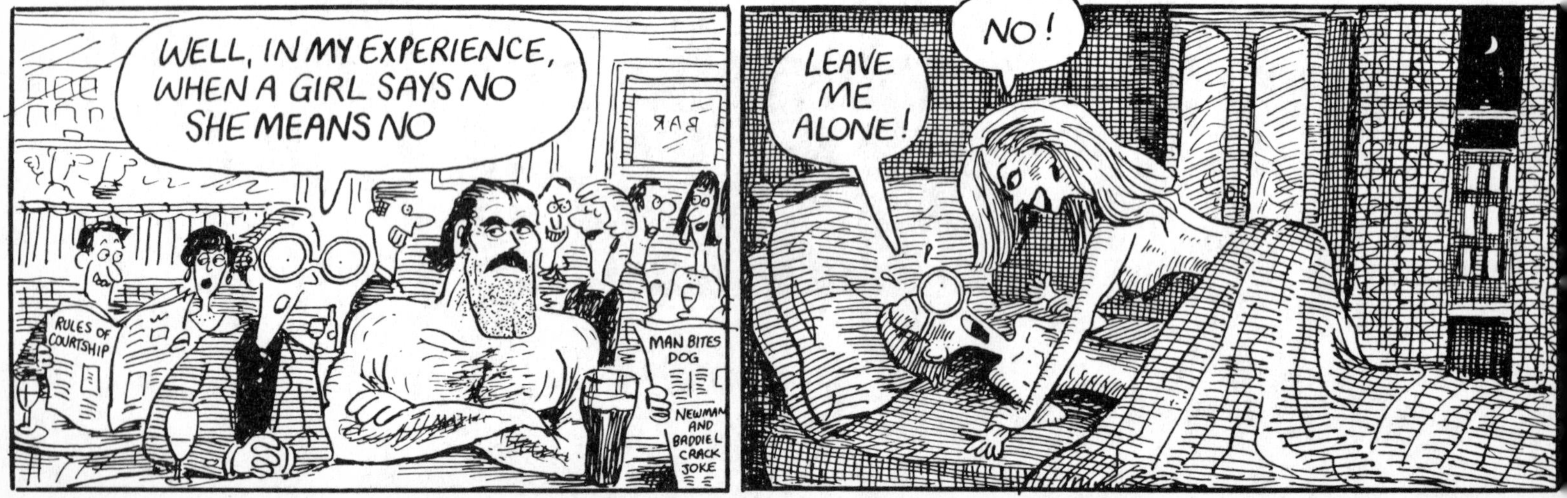
WELL, IN MY EXPERIENCE, WHEN A GIRL SAYS NO SHE MEANS NO
RULES OF COURTSHIP
MAN BITES DOG
NEWMAN AND BADDIEL CRACK JOKE
LEAVE ME ALONE!
NO!

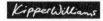

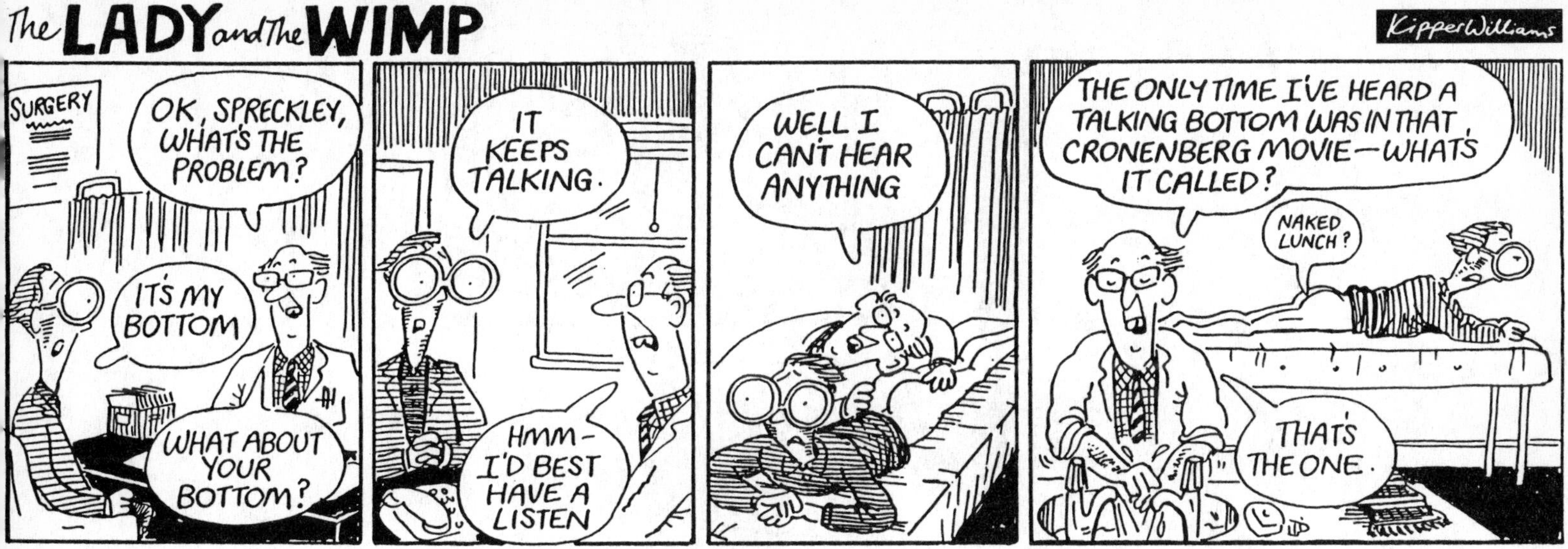
The LADY and The WIMP
Kipper Williams
SURGERY
OK, SPRECKLEY, WHAT'S THE PROBLEM?
IT'S MY BOTTOM
WHAT ABOUT YOUR BOTTOM?
IT KEEPS TALKING.
HMM- I'D BEST HAVE A LISTEN
WELL I CAN'T HEAR ANYTHING
THE ONLY TIME I'VE HEARD A TALKING BOTTOM WAS IN THAT CRONENBERG MOVIE—WHAT'S IT CALLED?
NAKED LUNCH?
THAT'S THE ONE.

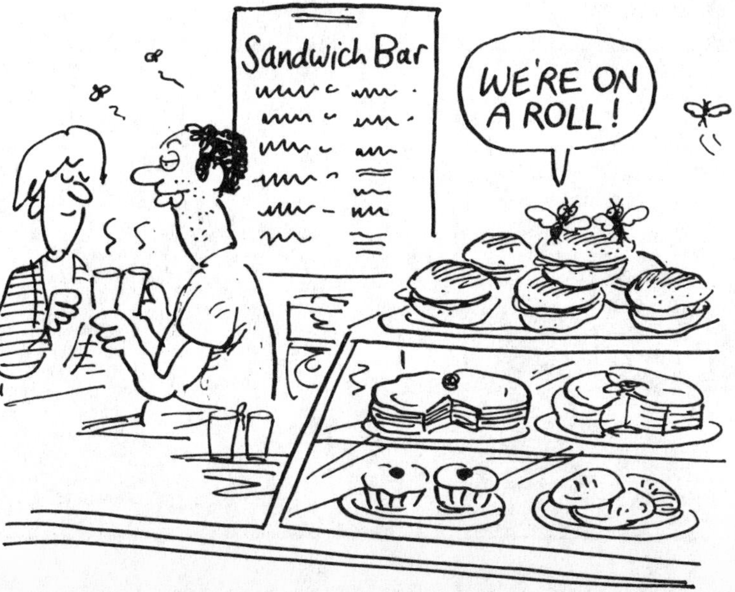
Sandwich Bar
WE'RE ON A ROLL!

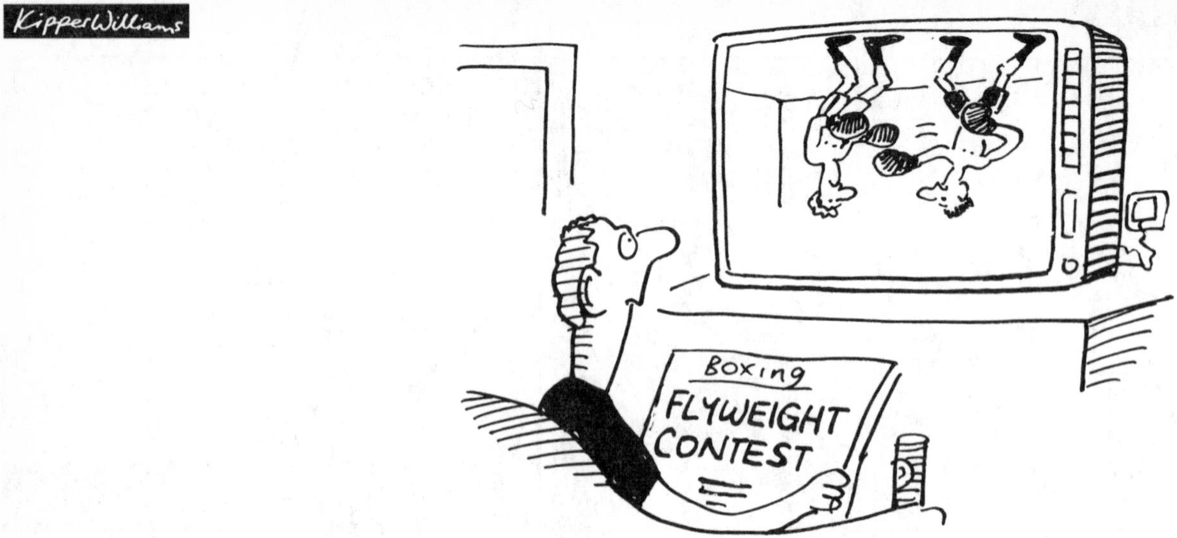
KipperWilliams
Boxing
FLYWEIGHT CONTEST

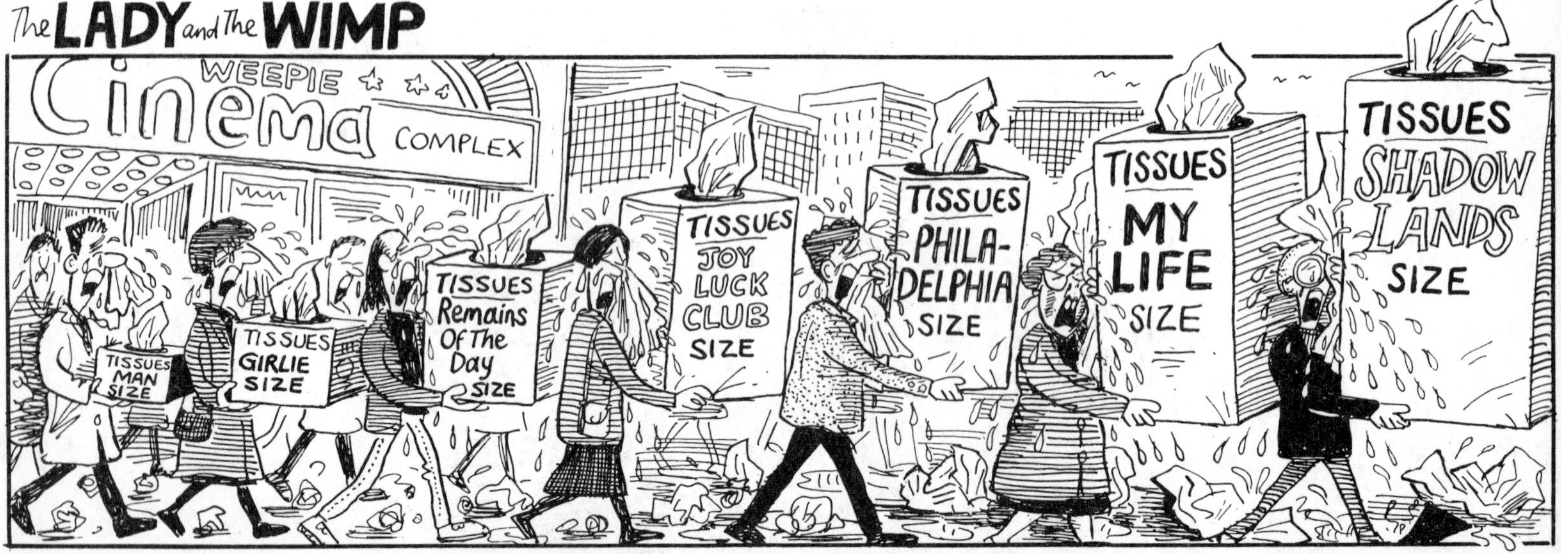
The LADY and The WIMP
WEEPIE
Cinema
COMPLEX
TISSUES MAN SIZE
TISSUES GIRLIE SIZE
TISSUES Remains Of The Day SIZE
TISSUES JOY LUCK CLUB SIZE
TISSUES PHILA-DELPHIA SIZE
TISSUES MY LIFE SIZE
TISSUES SHADOW LANDS SIZE

The LADY and The WIMP

Kipper Williams

AFTER BATEMAN

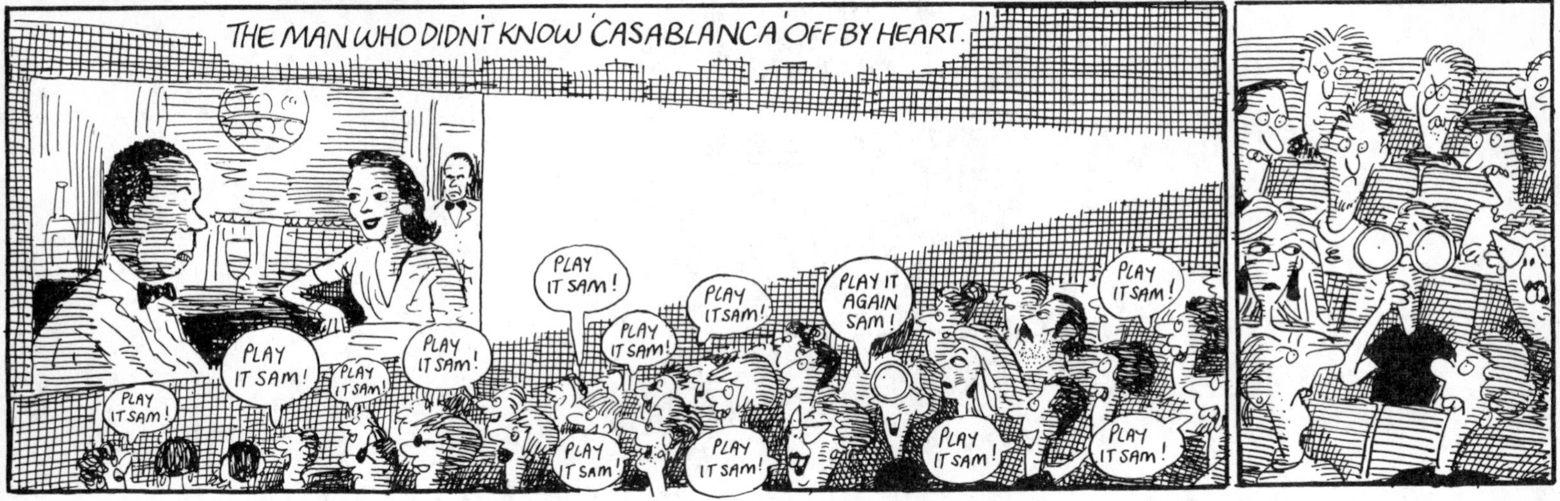

THE MAN WHO DIDN'T KNOW 'CASABLANCA' OFF BY HEART.
PLAY IT SAM!
PLAY IT SAM!
PLAY IT SAM!
PLAY IT SAM!
PLAY IT SAM!
PLAY IT SAM!
PLAY IT SAM!
PLAY IT SAM!
PLAY IT SAM!
PLAY IT AGAIN SAM!
PLAY IT SAM!
PLAY IT SAM!
PLAY IT SAM!

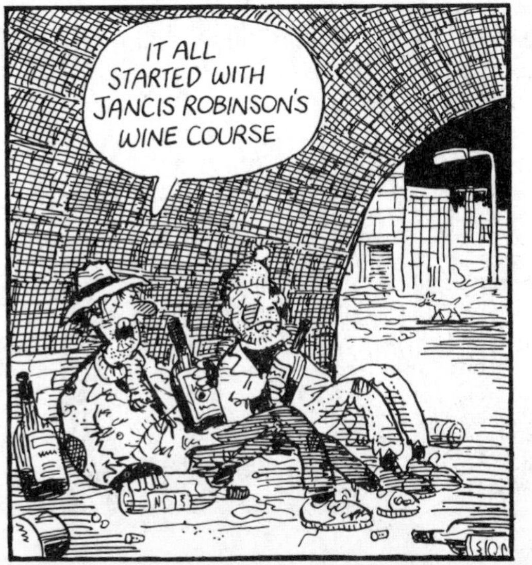

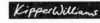

IT ALL STARTED WITH JANCIS ROBINSON'S WINE COURSE

KipperWilliams

ODEON
AROUND THE WORLD IN 80 ACCENTS

'It's Meryl Streep's latest.'

The LADY and The WIMP

THE MASK
POP CORN

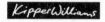

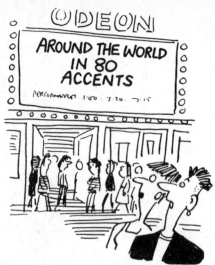

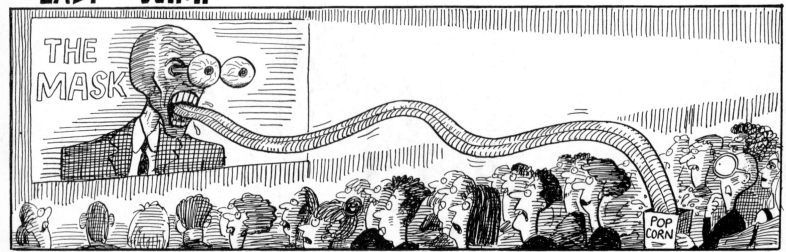

The LADY and The WIMP

Kipper Williams

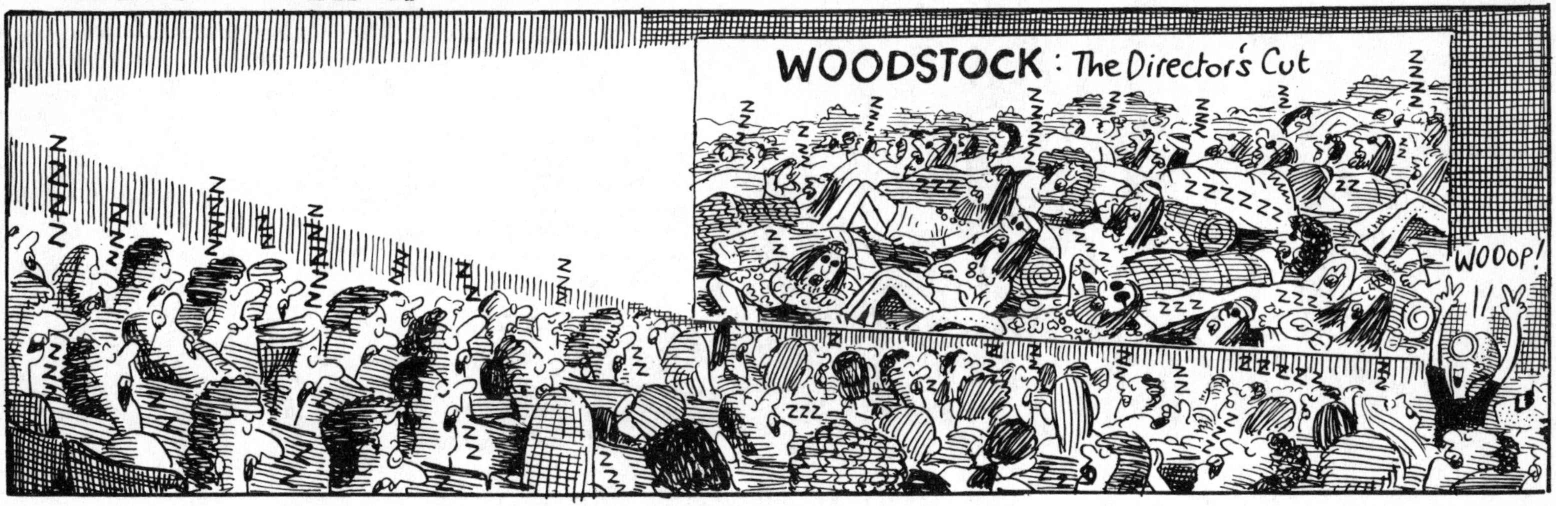
WOODSTOCK : The Director's Cut
WOOOP!

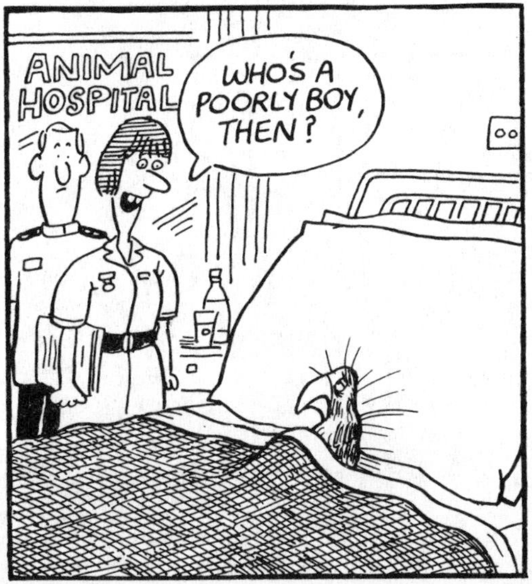
ANIMAL HOSPITAL
WHO'S A POORLY BOY, THEN?

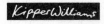

Kipper Williams

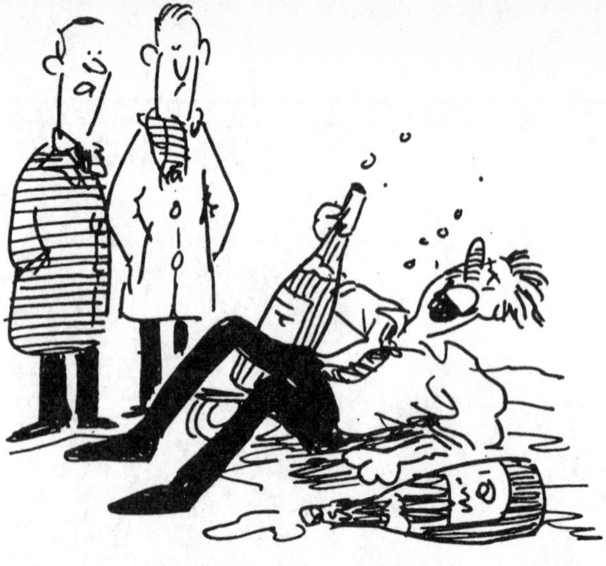

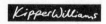

'There's méthode champenoise in his madness.'

The LADY and The WIMP

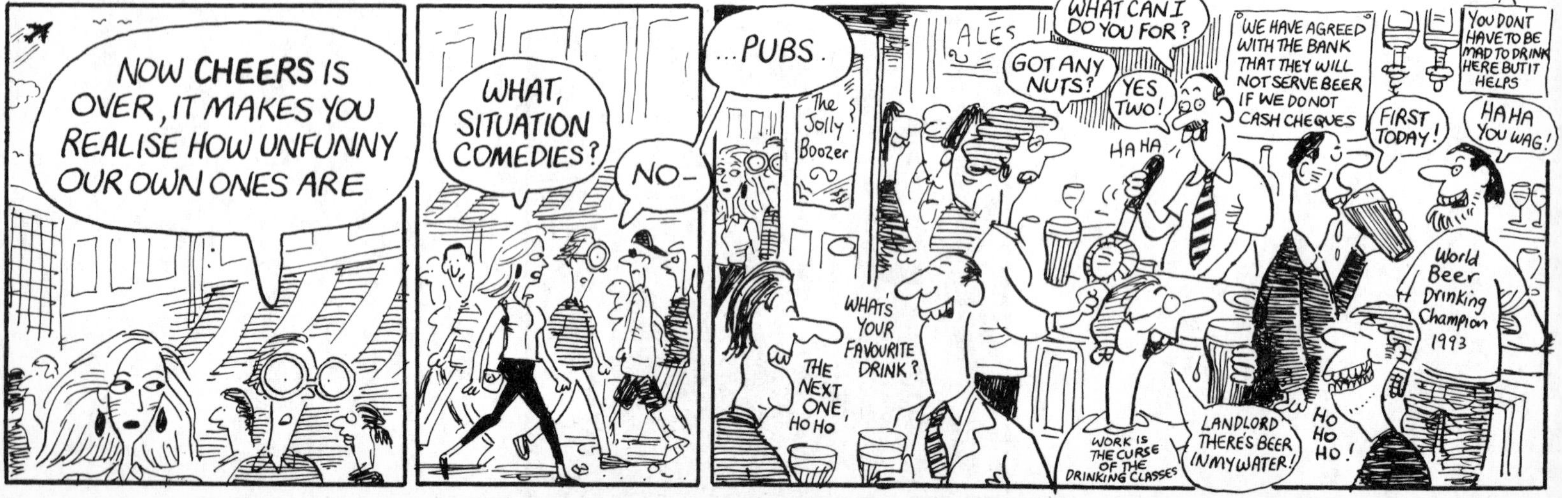
NOW CHEERS IS OVER, IT MAKES YOU REALISE HOW UNFUNNY OUR OWN ONES ARE
WHAT, SITUATION COMEDIES?
NO-
...PUBS.
ALES
The Jolly Boozer
GOT ANY NUTS?
WHAT CAN I DO YOU FOR?
YES TWO!
HA HA
WE HAVE AGREED WITH THE BANK THAT THEY WILL NOT SERVE BEER IF WE DO NOT CASH CHEQUES
FIRST TODAY!
YOU DONT HAVE TO BE MAD TO DRINK HERE BUT IT HELPS
HA HA YOU WAG!
World Beer Drinking Champion 1993
WHAT'S YOUR FAVOURITE DRINK?
THE NEXT ONE, HO HO
WORK IS THE CURSE OF THE DRINKING CLASSES
LANDLORD THERE'S BEER IN MY WATER!
HO HO HO!

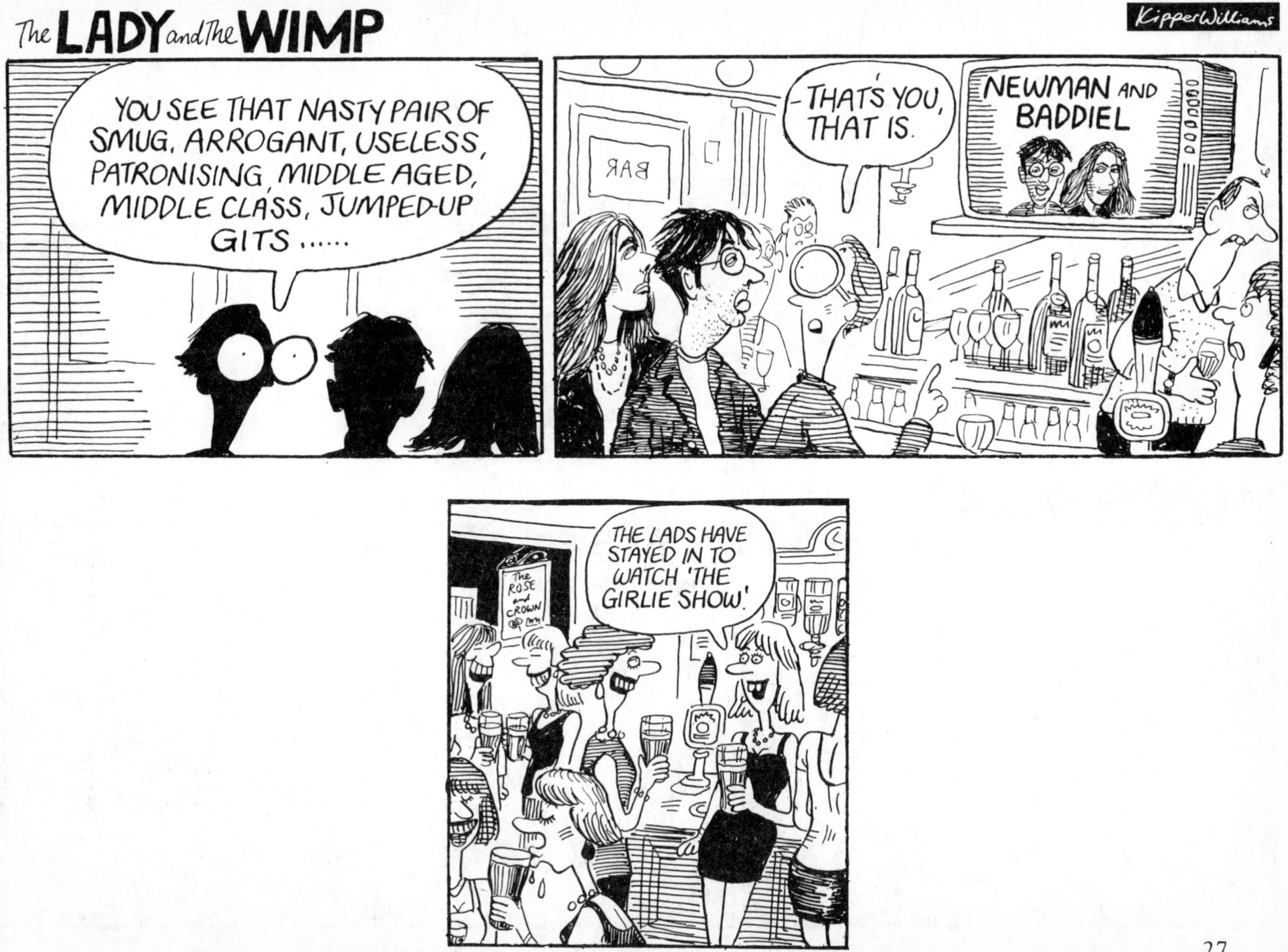
The LADY and The WIMP
Kipper Williams
YOU SEE THAT NASTY PAIR OF SMUG, ARROGANT, USELESS, PATRONISING, MIDDLE AGED, MIDDLE CLASS, JUMPED-UP GITS ......
- THAT'S YOU, THAT IS.
NEWMAN AND BADDIEL
BAR
THE LADS HAVE STAYED IN TO WATCH 'THE GIRLIE SHOW'.
The ROSE and CROWN

Kipper Williams

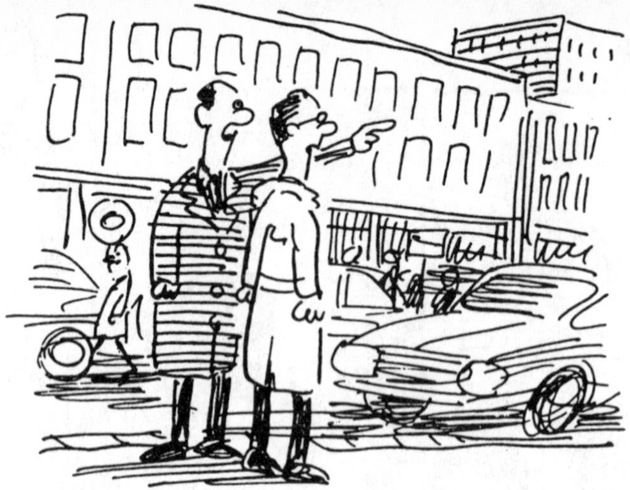

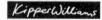

'Left at the charity shop, past the charity shop, second right after the charity shop . . .'

The LADY and The WIMP

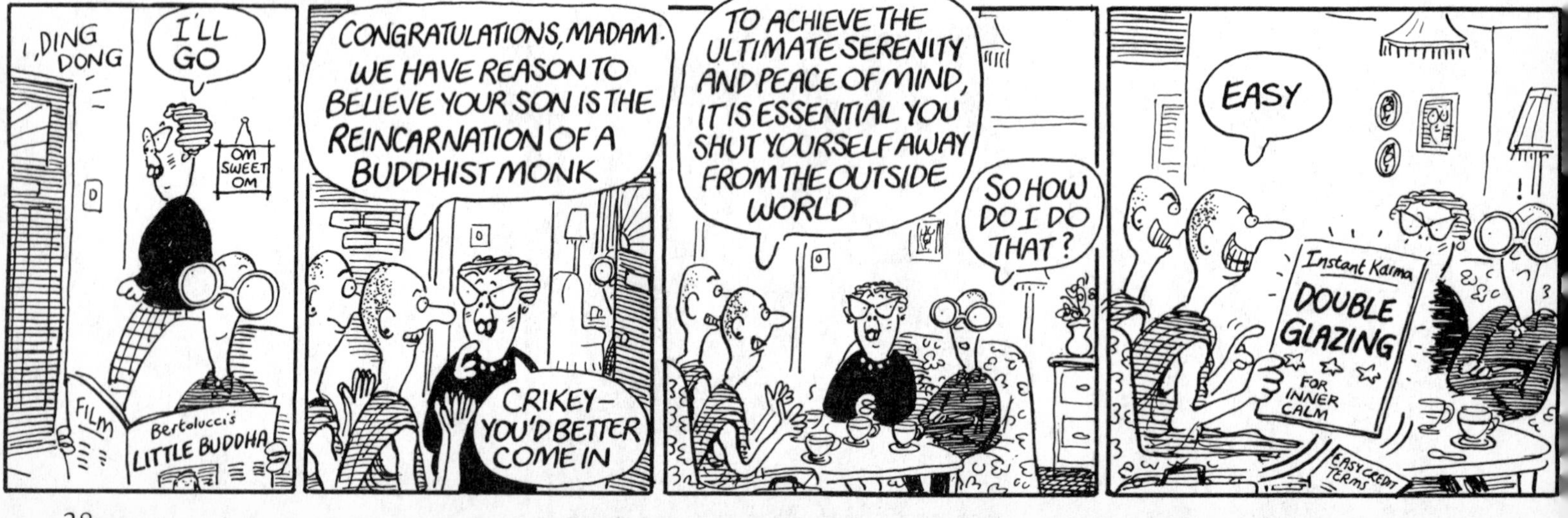

DING DONG
I'LL GO
OM SWEET OM
FILM
Bertolucci's LITTLE BUDDHA
CONGRATULATIONS, MADAM. WE HAVE REASON TO BELIEVE YOUR SON IS THE REINCARNATION OF A BUDDHIST MONK
CRIKEY— YOU'D BETTER COME IN
TO ACHIEVE THE ULTIMATE SERENITY AND PEACE OF MIND, IT IS ESSENTIAL YOU SHUT YOURSELF AWAY FROM THE OUTSIDE WORLD
SO HOW DO I DO THAT?
EASY
Instant Karma
DOUBLE GLAZING
FOR INNER CALM
EASY CREDIT TERMS

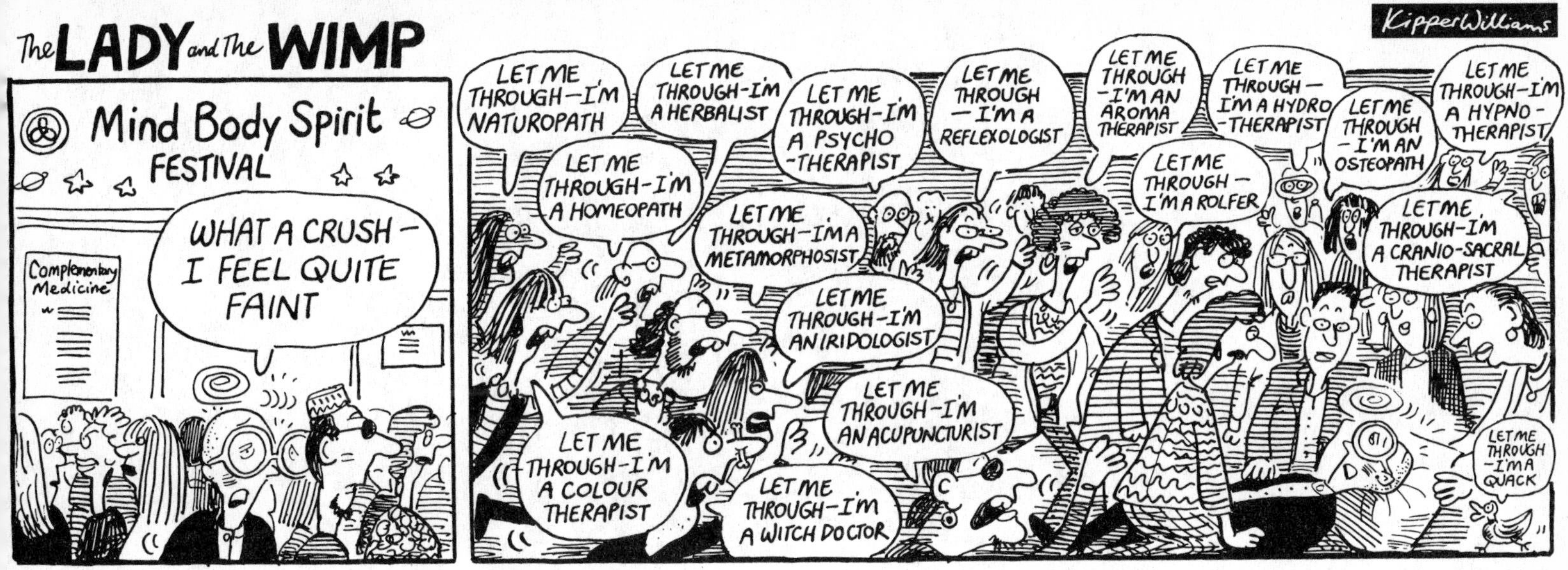

The LADY and The WIMP
Kipper Williams
Mind Body Spirit
FESTIVAL
Complementary Medicine
WHAT A CRUSH - I FEEL QUITE FAINT
LET ME THROUGH-I'M NATUROPATH
LET ME THROUGH-I'M A HERBALIST
LET ME THROUGH-I'M A PSYCHO-THERAPIST
LET ME THROUGH -I'M A REFLEXOLOGIST
LET ME THROUGH -I'M AN AROMA THERAPIST
LET ME THROUGH - I'M A HYDRO-THERAPIST
LET ME THROUGH -I'M AN OSTEOPATH
LET ME THROUGH-I'M A HYPNO-THERAPIST
LET ME THROUGH-I'M A HOMEOPATH
LET ME THROUGH-I'M A METAMORPHOSIST
LET ME THROUGH - I'M A ROLFER
LET ME THROUGH-I'M A CRANIO-SACRAL THERAPIST
LET ME THROUGH-I'M AN IRIDOLOGIST
LET ME THROUGH-I'M AN ACUPUNCTURIST
LET ME THROUGH-I'M A COLOUR THERAPIST
LET ME THROUGH-I'M A WITCH DOCTOR
LET ME THROUGH -I'M A QUACK

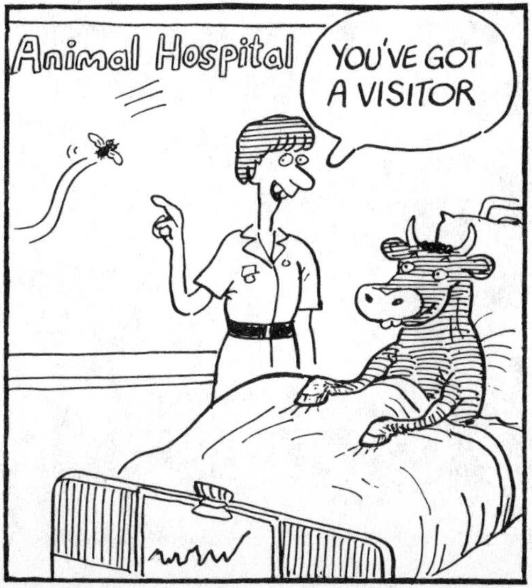

Animal Hospital
YOU'VE GOT A VISITOR

Kipper Williams

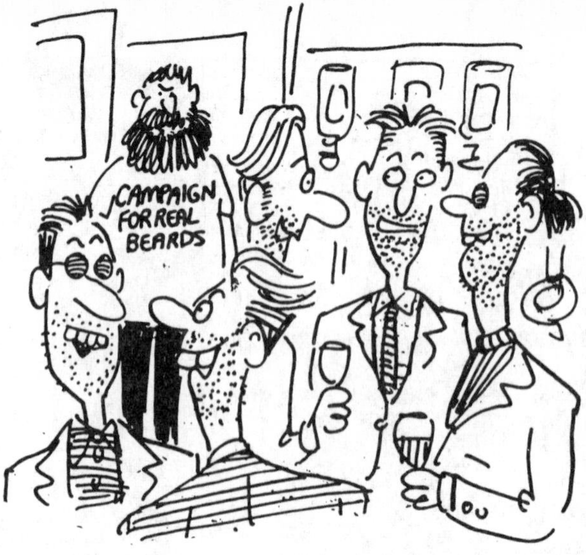
CAMPAIGN FOR REAL BEARDS

The LADY and The WIMP

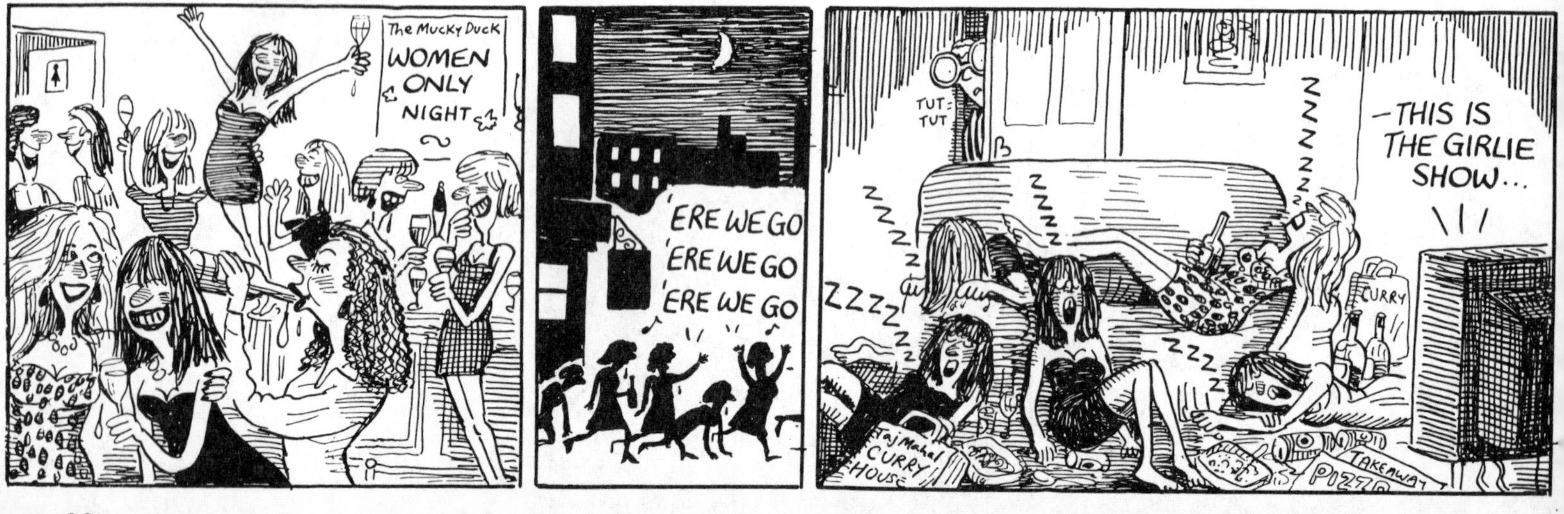
The Mucky Duck
WOMEN ONLY NIGHT
'ERE WE GO
'ERE WE GO
'ERE WE GO
TUT TUT
-THIS IS THE GIRLIE SHOW...
CURRY
Taj Mahal CURRY HOUS
TAKEAWAY
PIZZ

The LADY and The WIMP

Kipper Williams

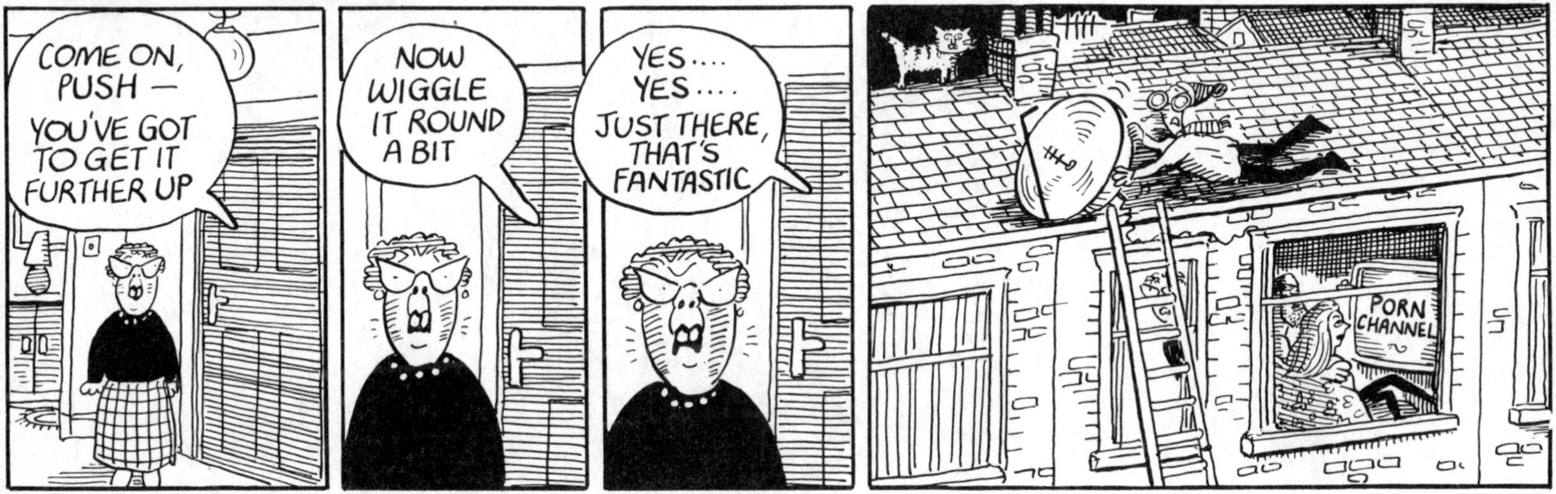
COME ON, PUSH — YOU'VE GOT TO GET IT FURTHER UP
NOW WIGGLE IT ROUND A BIT
YES.... YES.... JUST THERE, THAT'S FANTASTIC
PORN CHANNEL

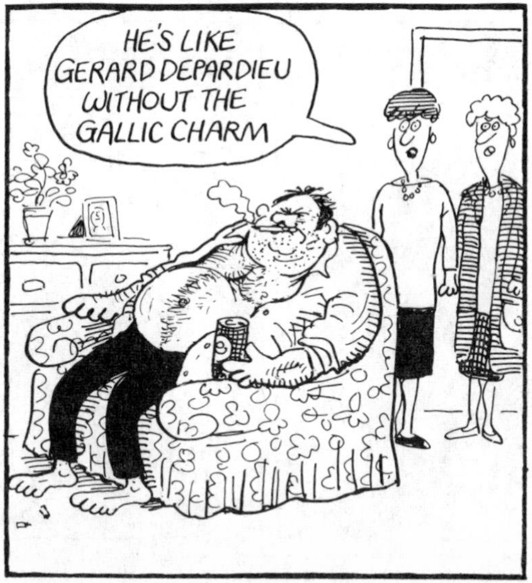
HE'S LIKE GERARD DEPARDIEU WITHOUT THE GALLIC CHARM

Kipper Williams

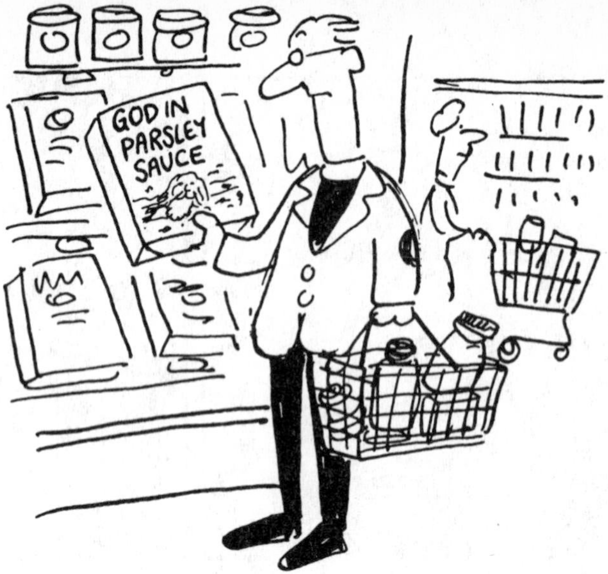
GOD IN PARSLEY SAUCE

The LADY and The WIMP

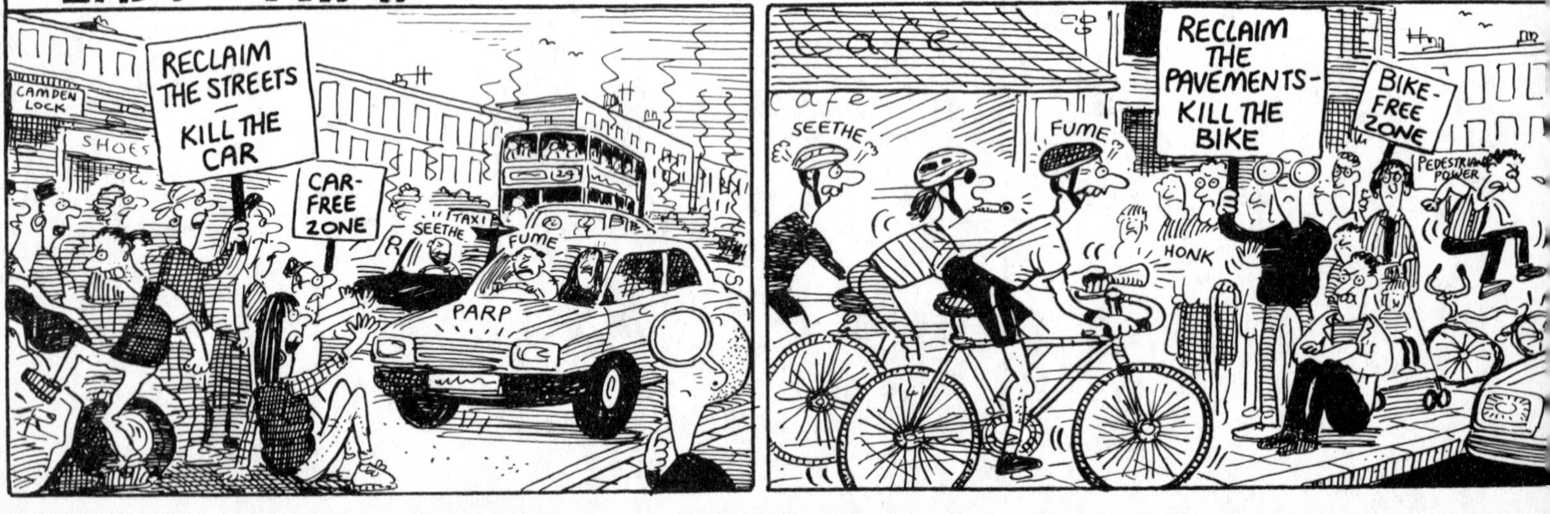
CAMDEN LOCK
SHOES
RECLAIM THE STREETS — KILL THE CAR
CAR-FREE ZONE
TAXI
SEETHE
FUME
PARP
Cafe
SEETHE
FUME
HONK
RECLAIM THE PAVEMENTS- KILL THE BIKE
BIKE-FREE ZONE
PEDESTRIAN POWER

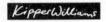

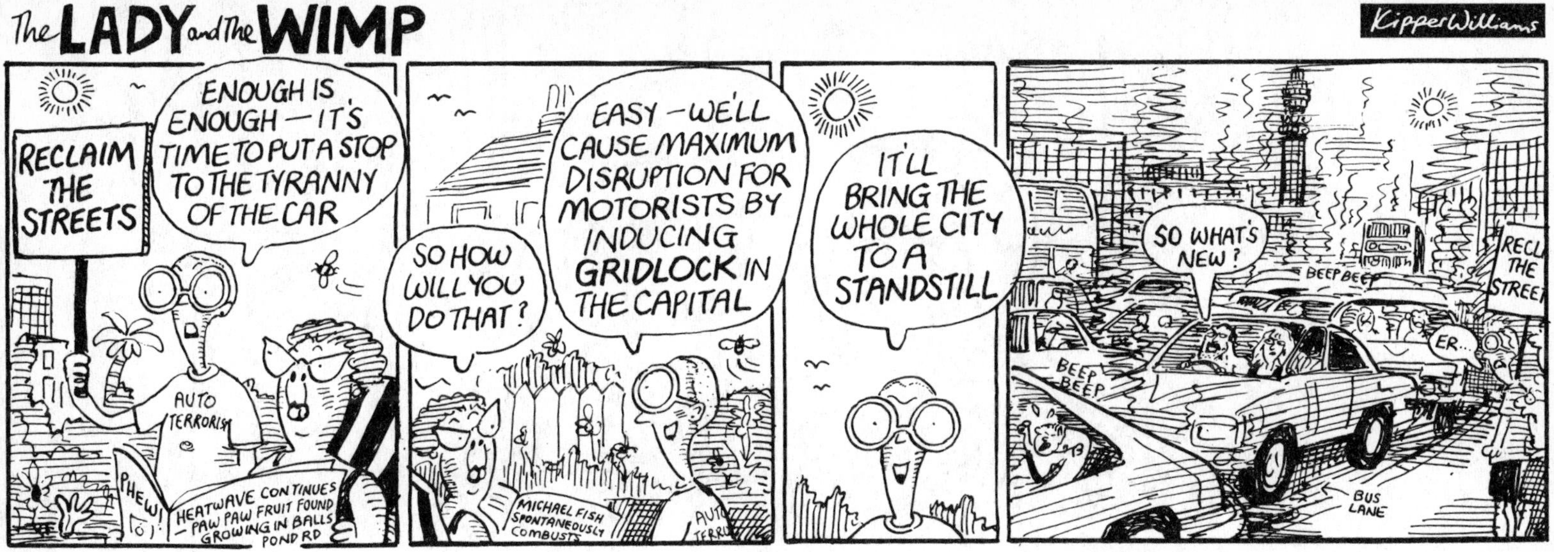
The LADY and The WIMP
KipperWilliams
RECLAIM THE STREETS
ENOUGH IS ENOUGH — IT'S TIME TO PUT A STOP TO THE TYRANNY OF THE CAR
AUTO TERRORIST
PHEW!
HEATWAVE CONTINUES — PAW PAW FRUIT FOUND GROWING IN BALLS POND RD
SO HOW WILL YOU DO THAT?
EASY — WE'LL CAUSE MAXIMUM DISRUPTION FOR MOTORISTS BY INDUCING GRIDLOCK IN THE CAPITAL
MICHAEL FISH SPONTANEOUSLY COMBUSTS
IT'LL BRING THE WHOLE CITY TO A STANDSTILL
SO WHAT'S NEW?
BEEP BEEP
BEEP BEEP
ER...
BUS LANE

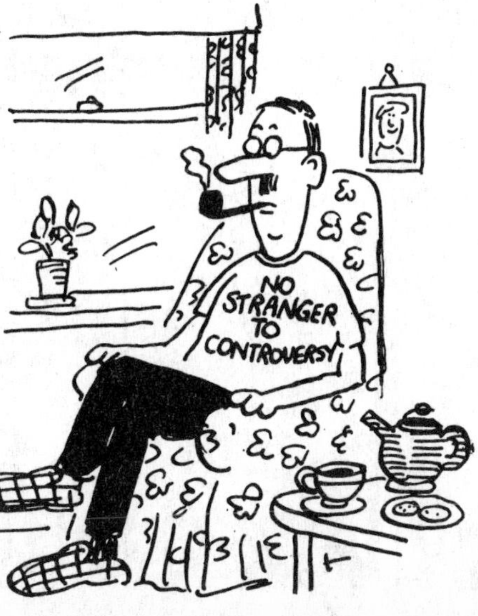
NO STRANGER TO CONTROVERSY

Kipper Williams

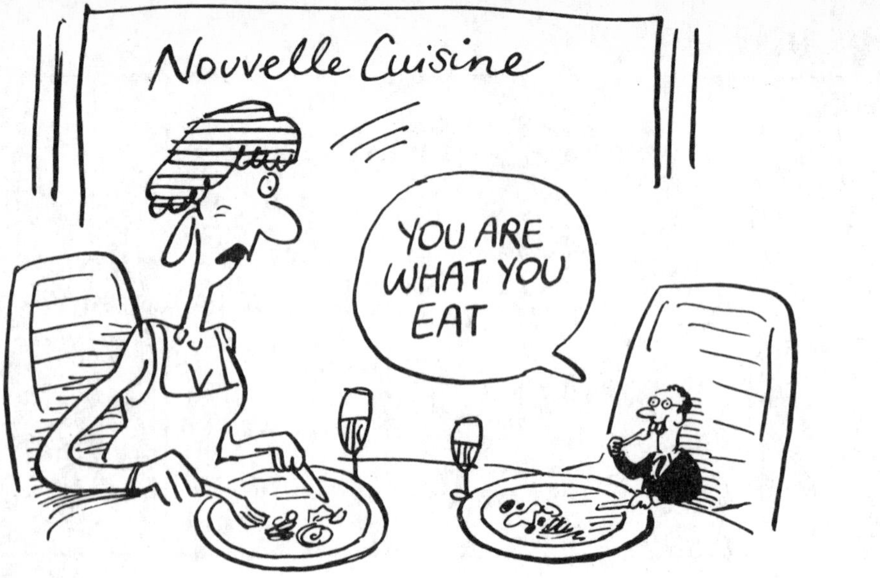
Nouvelle Cuisine
YOU ARE WHAT YOU EAT

The LADY and The WIMP

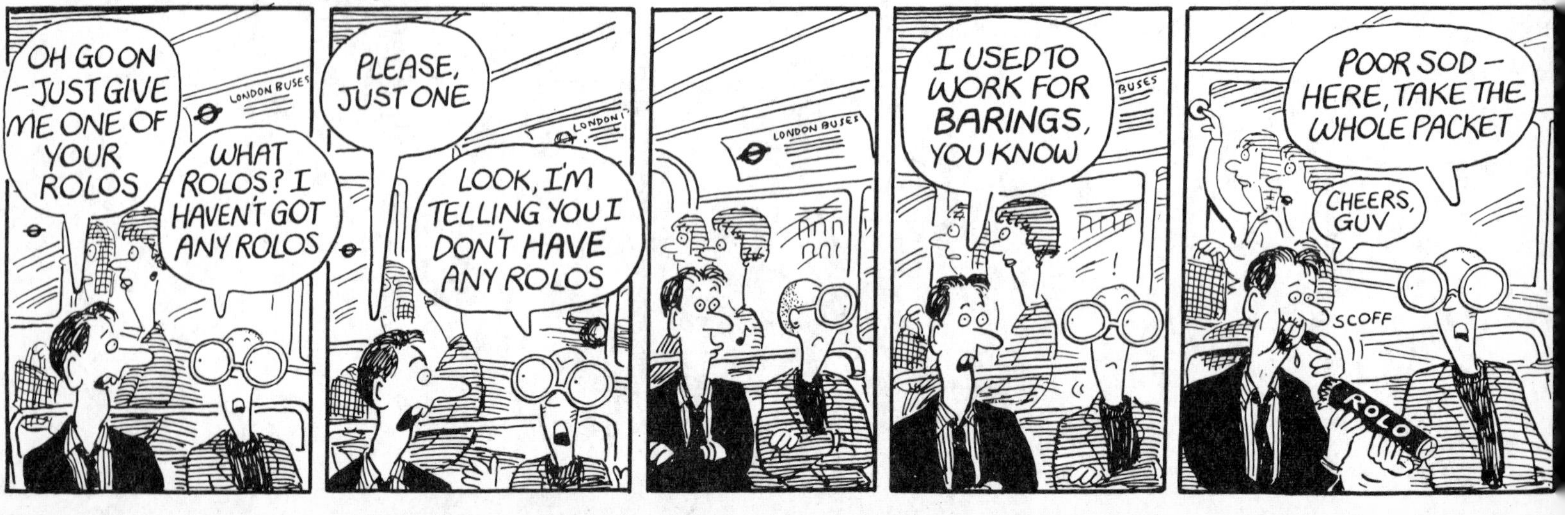
OH GO ON - JUST GIVE ME ONE OF YOUR ROLOS
LONDON BUSES
WHAT ROLOS? I HAVEN'T GOT ANY ROLOS
PLEASE, JUST ONE
LOOK, I'M TELLING YOU I DON'T HAVE ANY ROLOS
LONDON BUSES
I USED TO WORK FOR BARINGS, YOU KNOW
BUSES
POOR SOD - HERE, TAKE THE WHOLE PACKET
CHEERS, GUV
SCOFF
ROLO

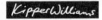

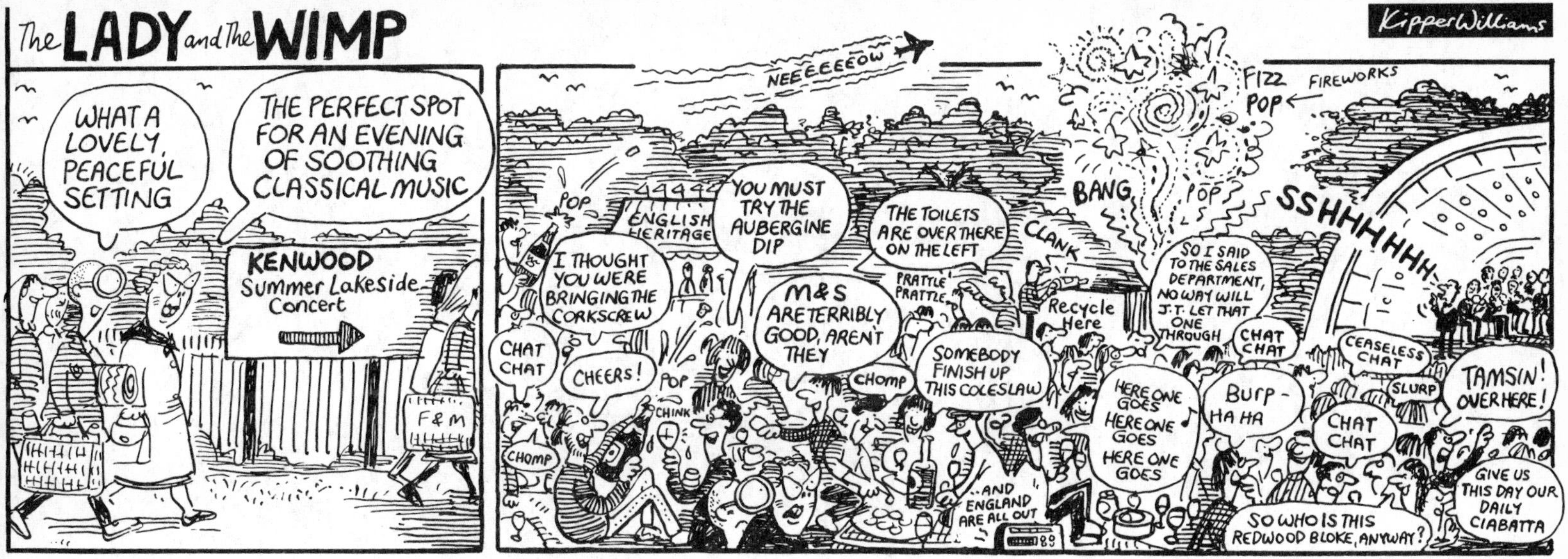
The LADY and The WIMP
Kipper Williams
WHAT A LOVELY, PEACEFUL SETTING
THE PERFECT SPOT FOR AN EVENING OF SOOTHING CLASSICAL MUSIC
KENWOOD Summer Lakeside Concert
F&M
NEEEEEEOW
FIZZ POP
FIREWORKS
POP
ENGLISH HERITAGE
YOU MUST TRY THE AUBERGINE DIP
THE TOILETS ARE OVER THERE ON THE LEFT
CLANK
BANG
POP
SSHHHHHH
I THOUGHT YOU WERE BRINGING THE CORKSCREW
PRATTLE PRATTLE
M&S ARE TERRIBLY GOOD, AREN'T THEY
Recycle Here
SO I SAID TO THE SALES DEPARTMENT, NO WAY WILL J.T. LET THAT ONE THROUGH
CHAT CHAT
CEASELESS CHAT
CHAT CHAT
CHEERS!
POP
CHINK
CHOMP
SOMEBODY FINISH UP THIS COLESLAW
HERE ONE GOES HERE ONE GOES HERE ONE GOES
BURP - HA HA
SLURP
TAMSIN! OVER HERE!
CHAT CHAT
CHOMP
...AND ENGLAND ARE ALL OUT
SO WHO IS THIS REDWOOD BLOKE, ANYWAY?
GIVE US THIS DAY OUR DAILY CIABATTA

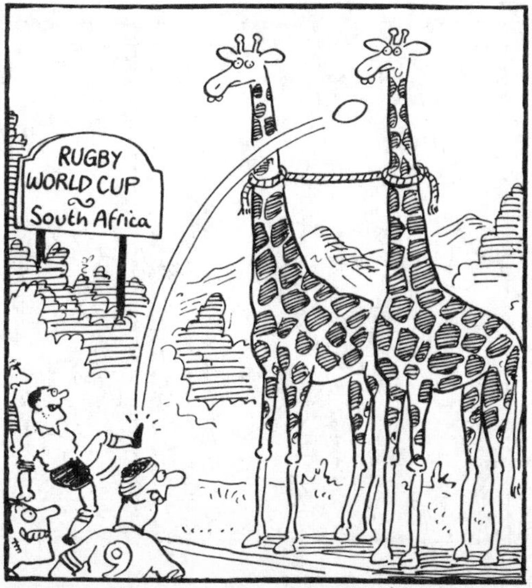
RUGBY WORLD CUP
South Africa

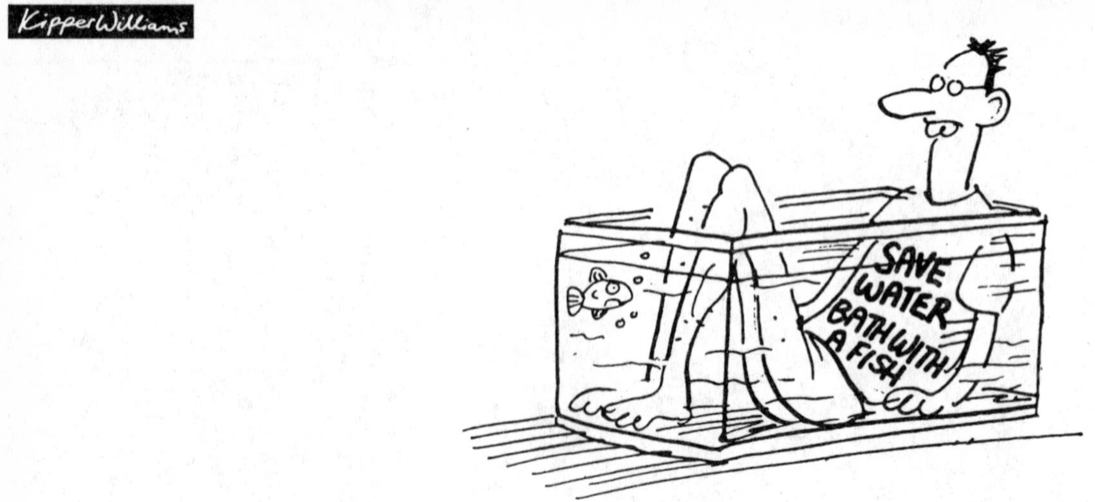
Kipper Williams
SAVE WATER BATH WITH A FISH

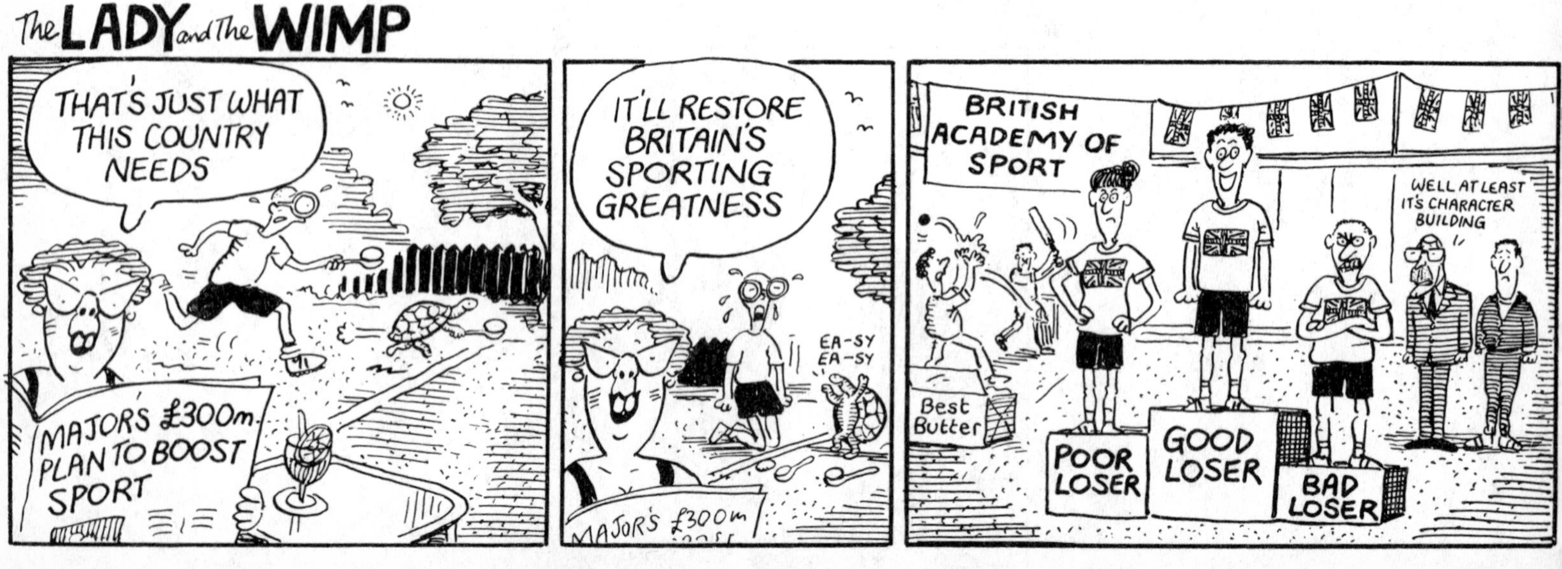
The LADY and The WIMP
THAT'S JUST WHAT THIS COUNTRY NEEDS
MAJOR'S £300m PLAN TO BOOST SPORT
IT'LL RESTORE BRITAIN'S SPORTING GREATNESS
EA-SY EA-SY
MAJOR'S £300m
BRITISH ACADEMY OF SPORT
WELL AT LEAST IT'S CHARACTER BUILDING
Best Butter
POOR LOSER
GOOD LOSER
BAD LOSER

The LADY and The WIMP

Kipper Williams

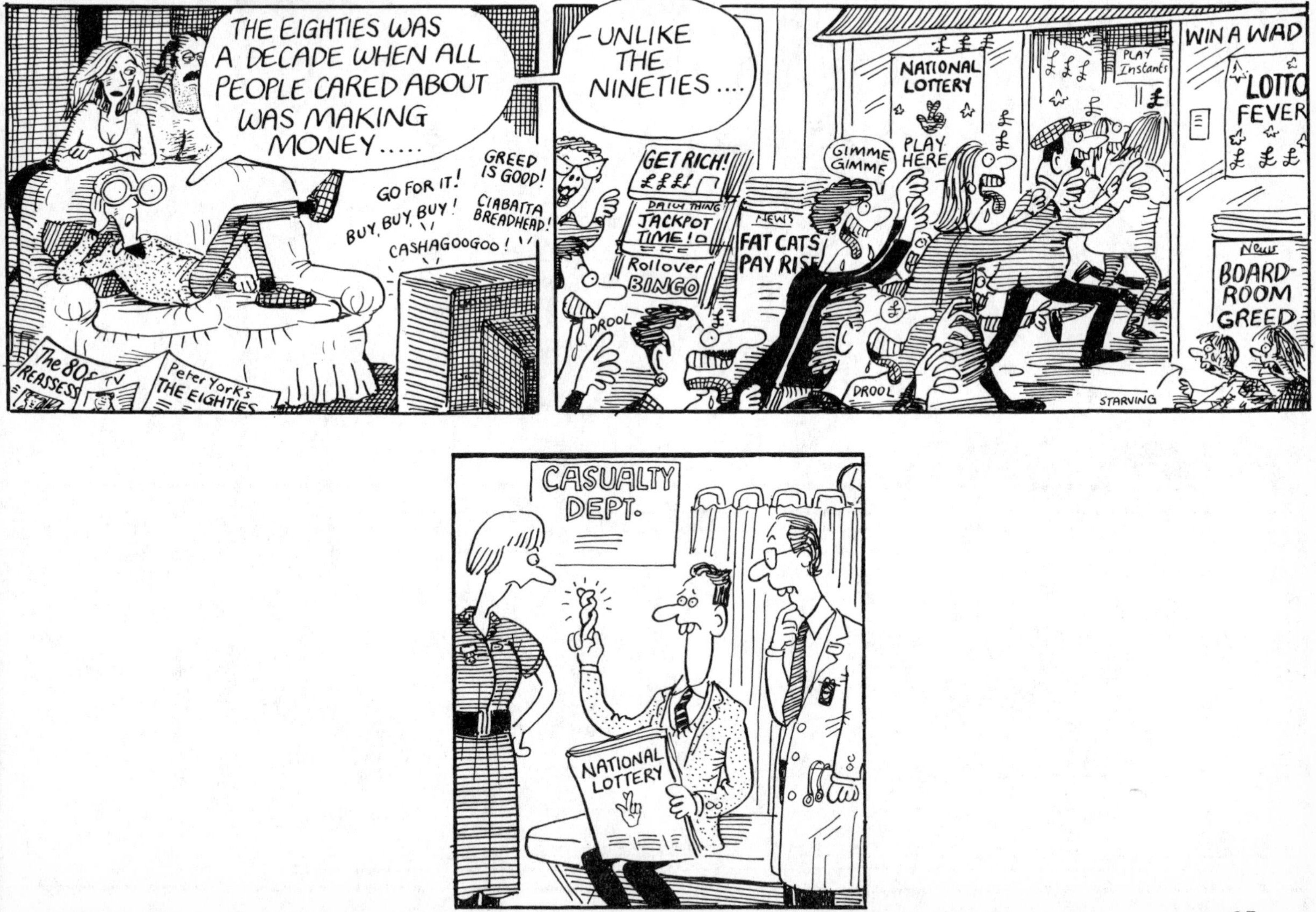

THE EIGHTIES WAS A DECADE WHEN ALL PEOPLE CARED ABOUT WAS MAKING MONEY.....
GO FOR IT!
BUY, BUY, BUY!
CASHAGOOGOO!
GREED IS GOOD!
CIABATTA BREADHEAD!
The 80s REASSESS
TV
Peter York's THE EIGHTIES
–UNLIKE THE NINETIES....
GET RICH! ££££
JACKPOT TIME!
Rollover BINGO
NEWS
FAT CATS PAY RISE
NATIONAL LOTTERY
PLAY HERE
GIMME GIMME
PLAY Instants
WIN A WAD
LOTTO FEVER
News
BOARD-ROOM GREED
DROOL
DROOL
STARVING
CASUALTY DEPT.
NATIONAL LOTTERY

KipperWilliams

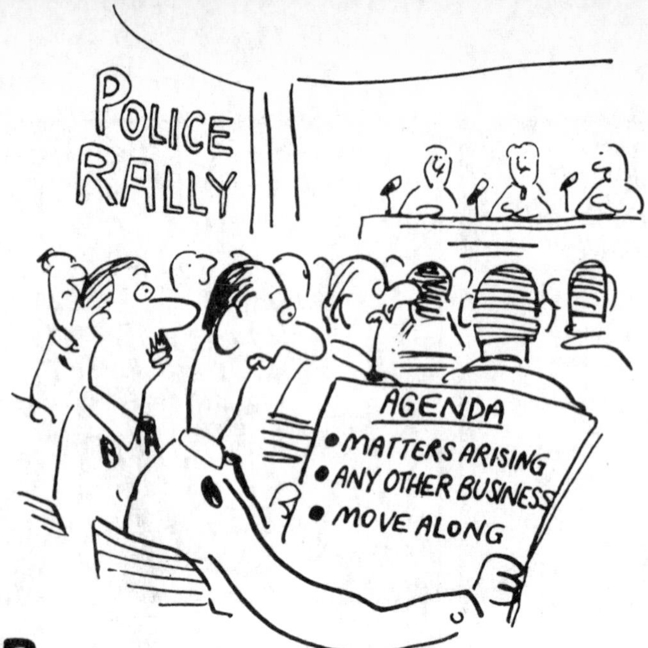
POLICE RALLY
AGENDA
• MATTERS ARISING
• ANY OTHER BUSINESS
• MOVE ALONG

The LADY and The WIMP

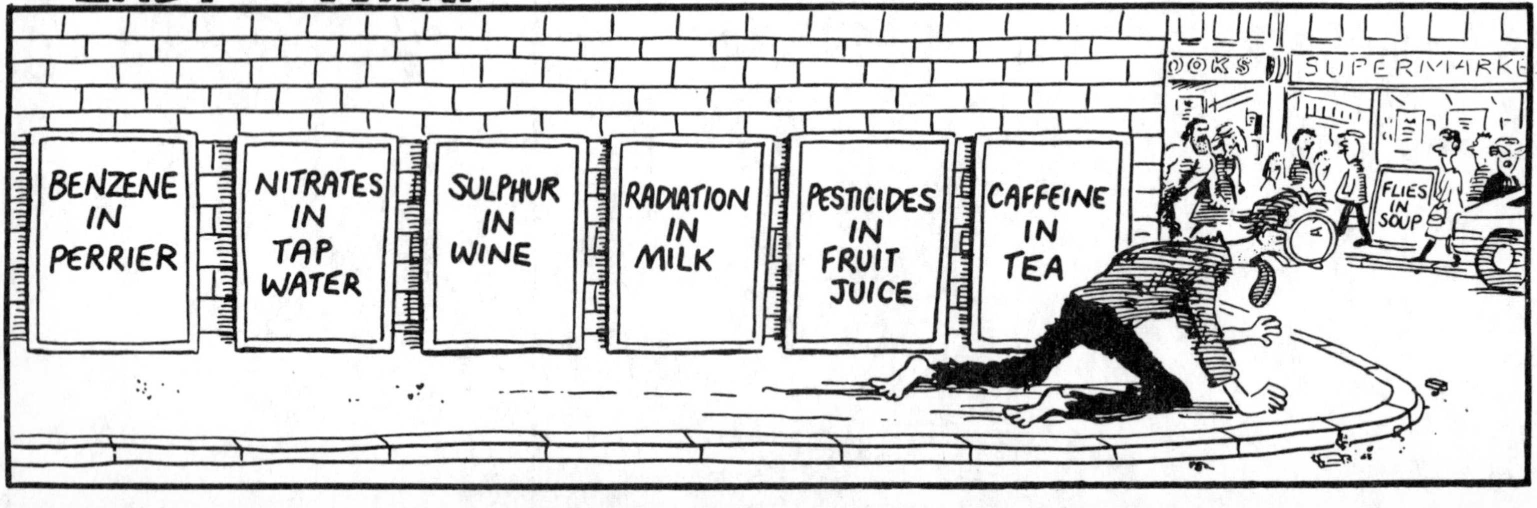
BENZENE IN PERRIER
NITRATES IN TAP WATER
SULPHUR IN WINE
RADIATION IN MILK
PESTICIDES IN FRUIT JUICE
CAFFEINE IN TEA
FLIES IN SOUP

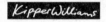

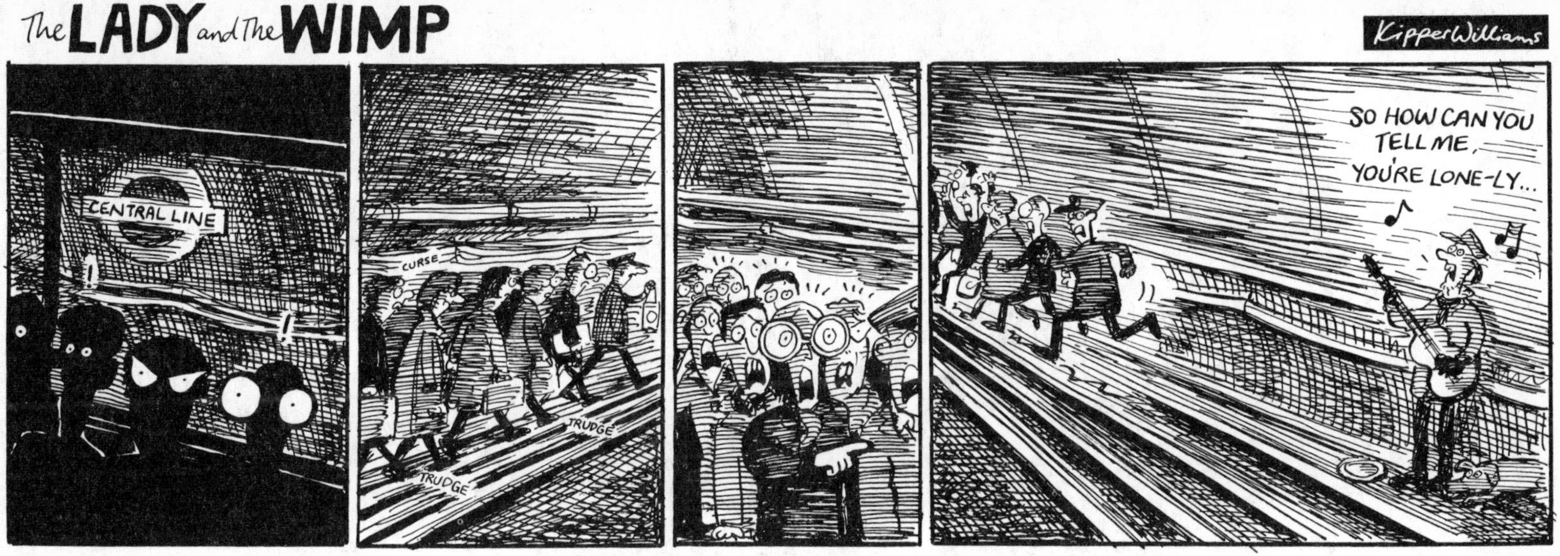
The LADY and The WIMP
Kipper Williams
CENTRAL LINE
CURSE
TRUDGE
TRUDGE
SO HOW CAN YOU TELL ME, YOU'RE LONE-LY...

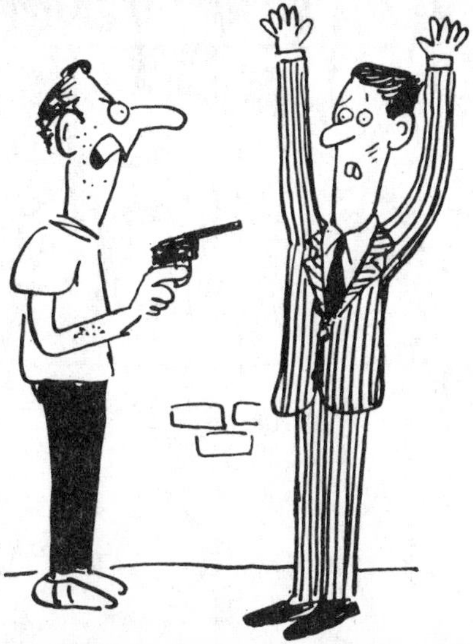

'Your money or your quality of life.'

Kipper Williams

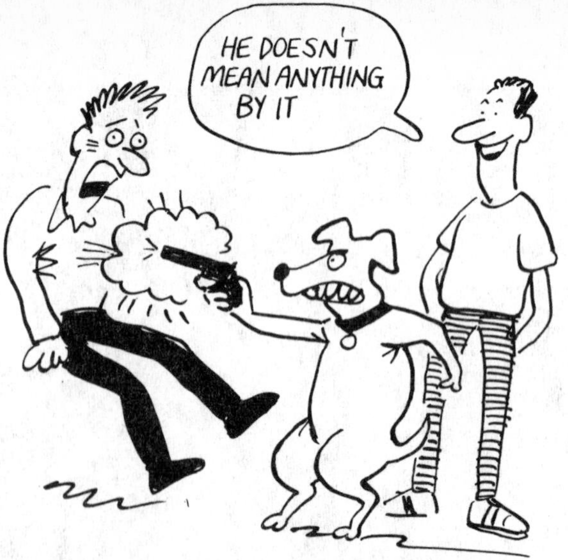
HE DOESN'T MEAN ANYTHING BY IT

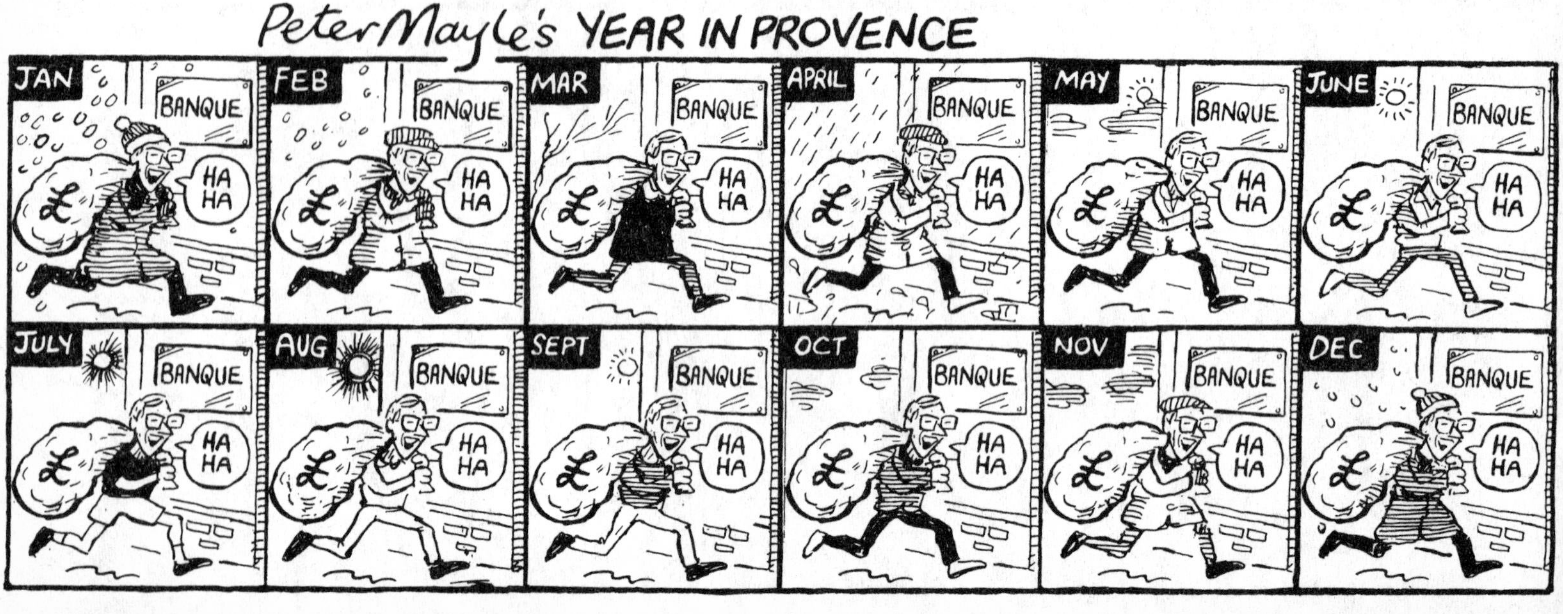
Peter Mayle's YEAR IN PROVENCE
JAN
BANQUE
HA HA
FEB
BANQUE
HA HA
MAR
BANQUE
HA HA
APRIL
BANQUE
HA HA
MAY
BANQUE
HA HA
JUNE
BANQUE
HA HA
JULY
BANQUE
HA HA
AUG
BANQUE
HA HA
SEPT
BANQUE
HA HA
OCT
BANQUE
HA HA
NOV
BANQUE
HA HA
DEC
BANQUE
HA HA

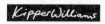

Kipper Williams

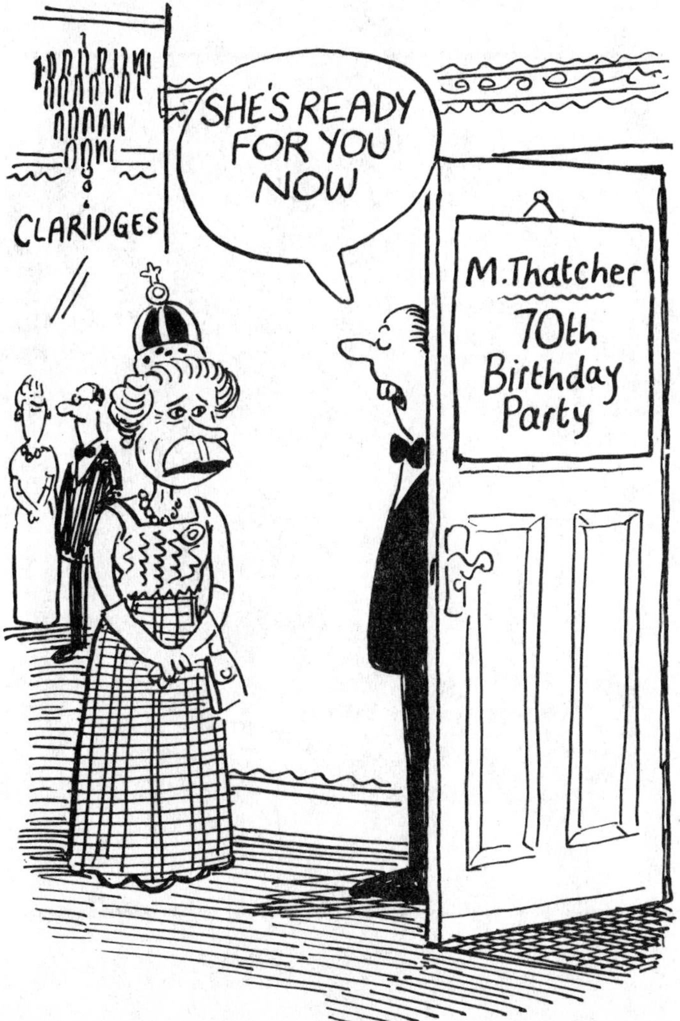
CLARIDGES
SHE'S READY FOR YOU NOW
M.Thatcher
70th Birthday Party

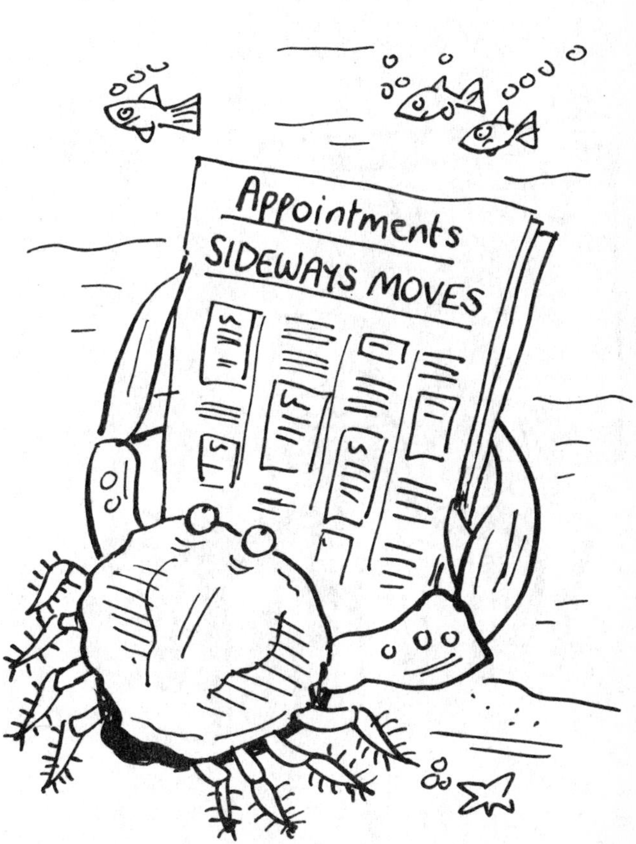
Appointments
SIDEWAYS MOVES

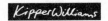

KipperWilliams

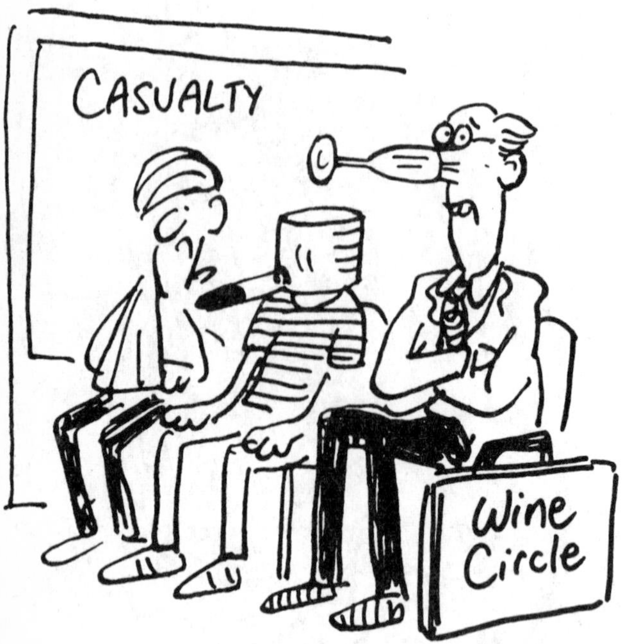
CASUALTY
Wine Circle

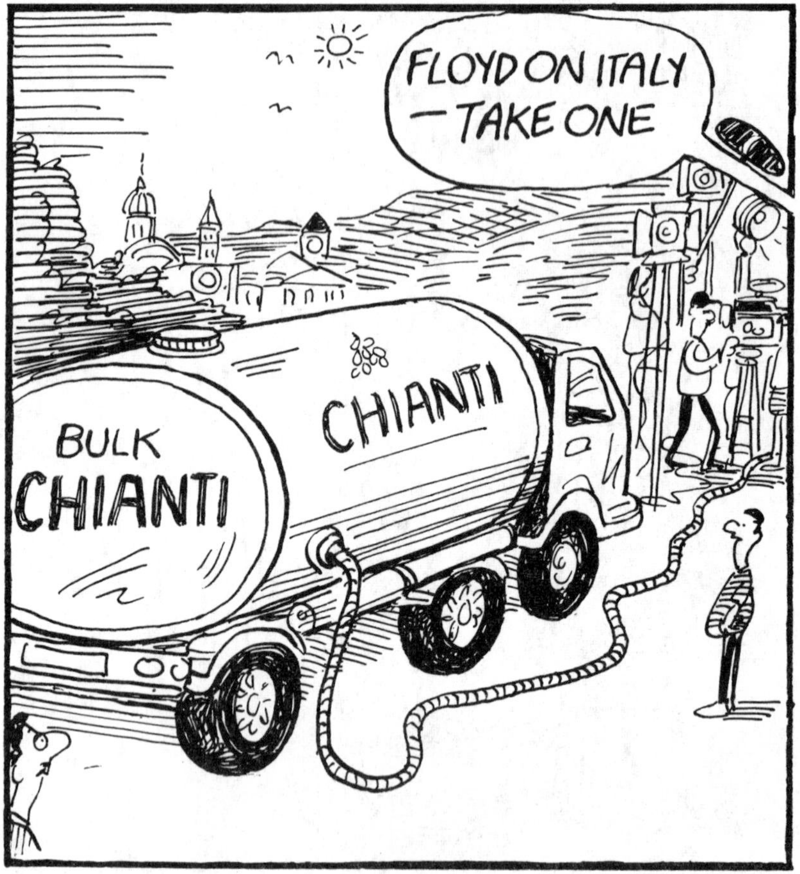
FLOYD ON ITALY — TAKE ONE
BULK CHIANTI
CHIANTI

KipperWilliams

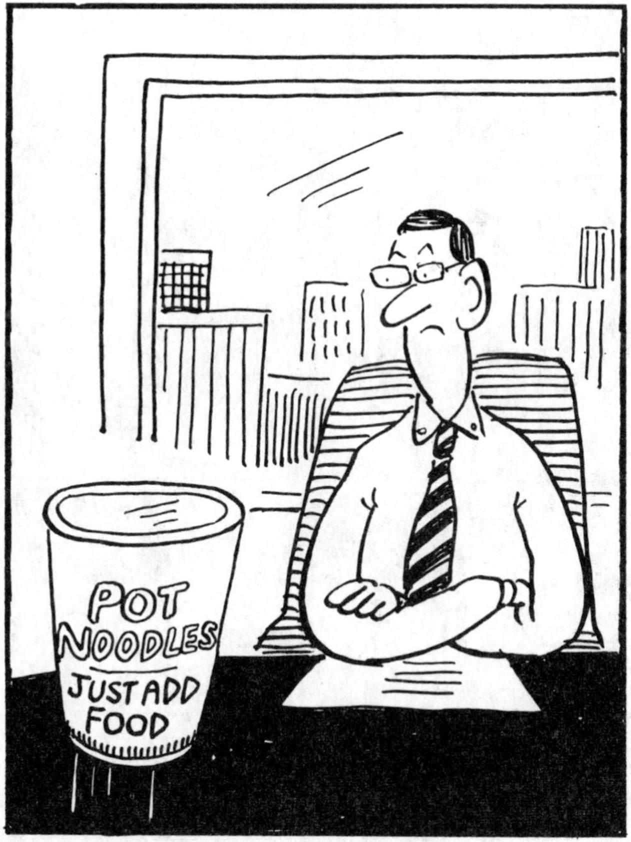
POT NOODLES
JUST ADD FOOD

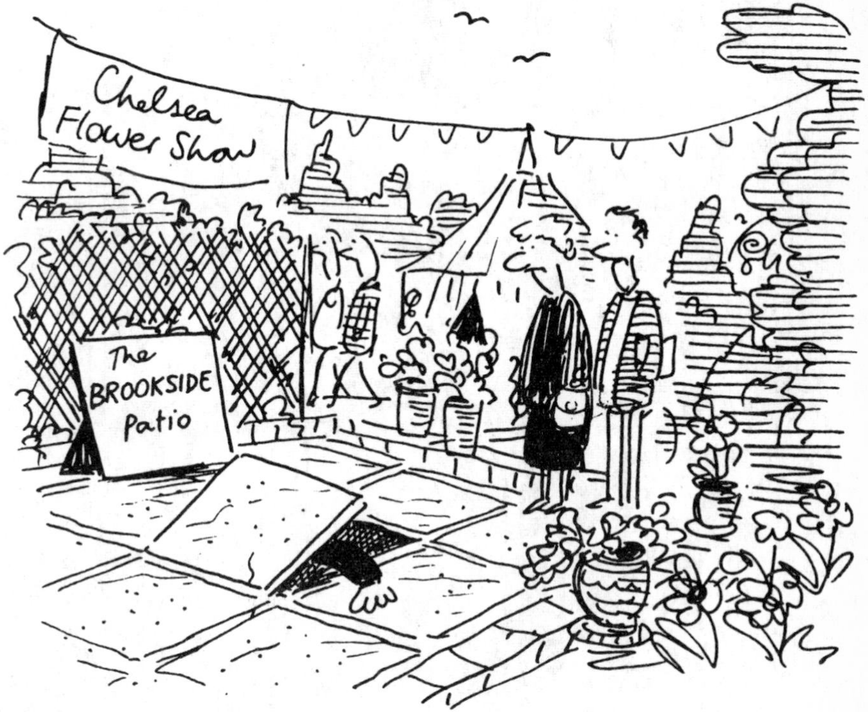
Chelsea Flower Show
The BROOKSIDE Patio

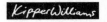

KipperWilliams

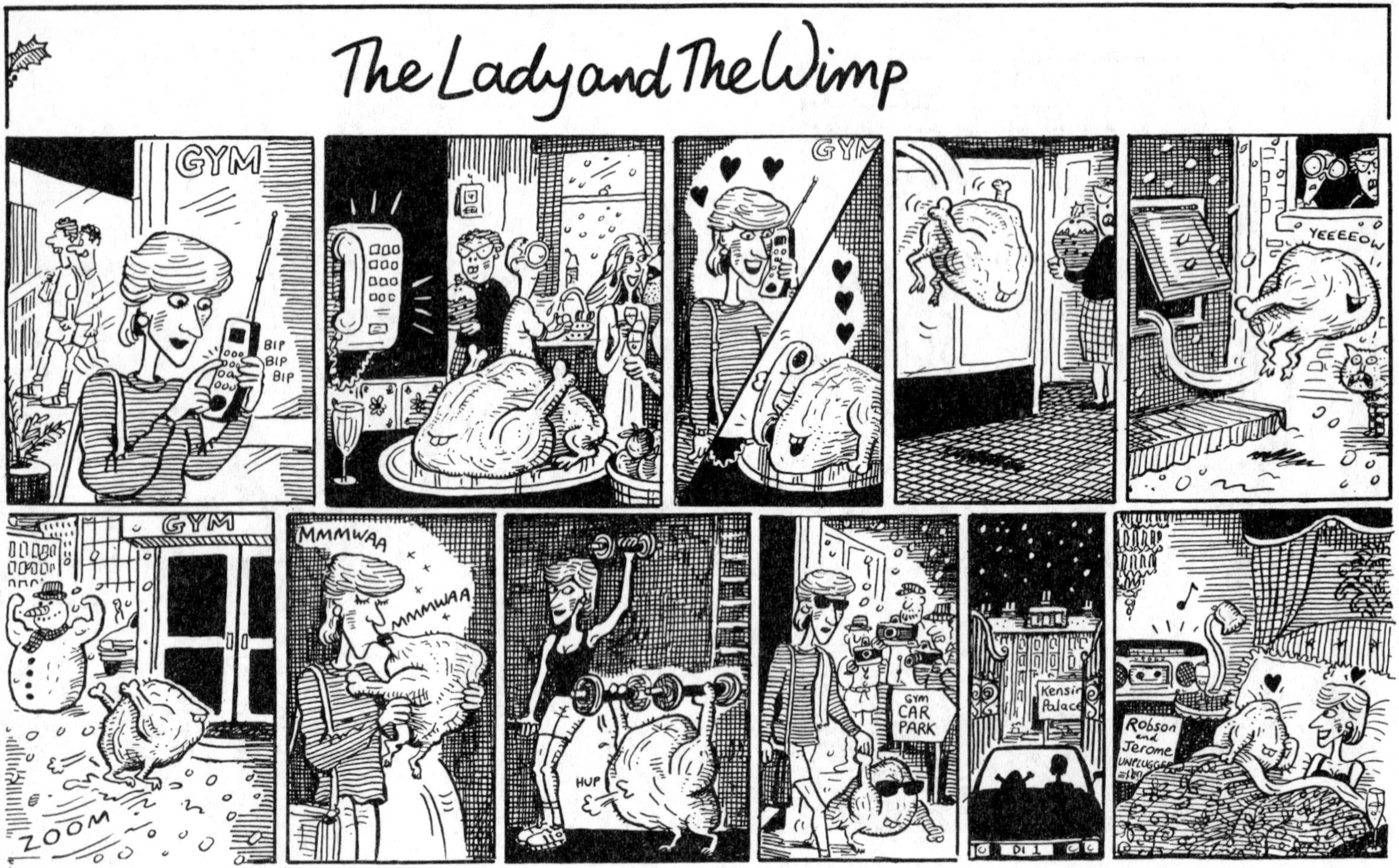
The Lady and The Wimp
GYM
BIP
BIP
BIP
GYM
YEEEEOW
GYM
ZOOM
MMMWAA
MMMWAA
HUP
GYM
CAR
PARK
Kensin
Palace
DI 1
Robson
and
Jerome

CONTINUED →

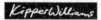

KipperWilliams

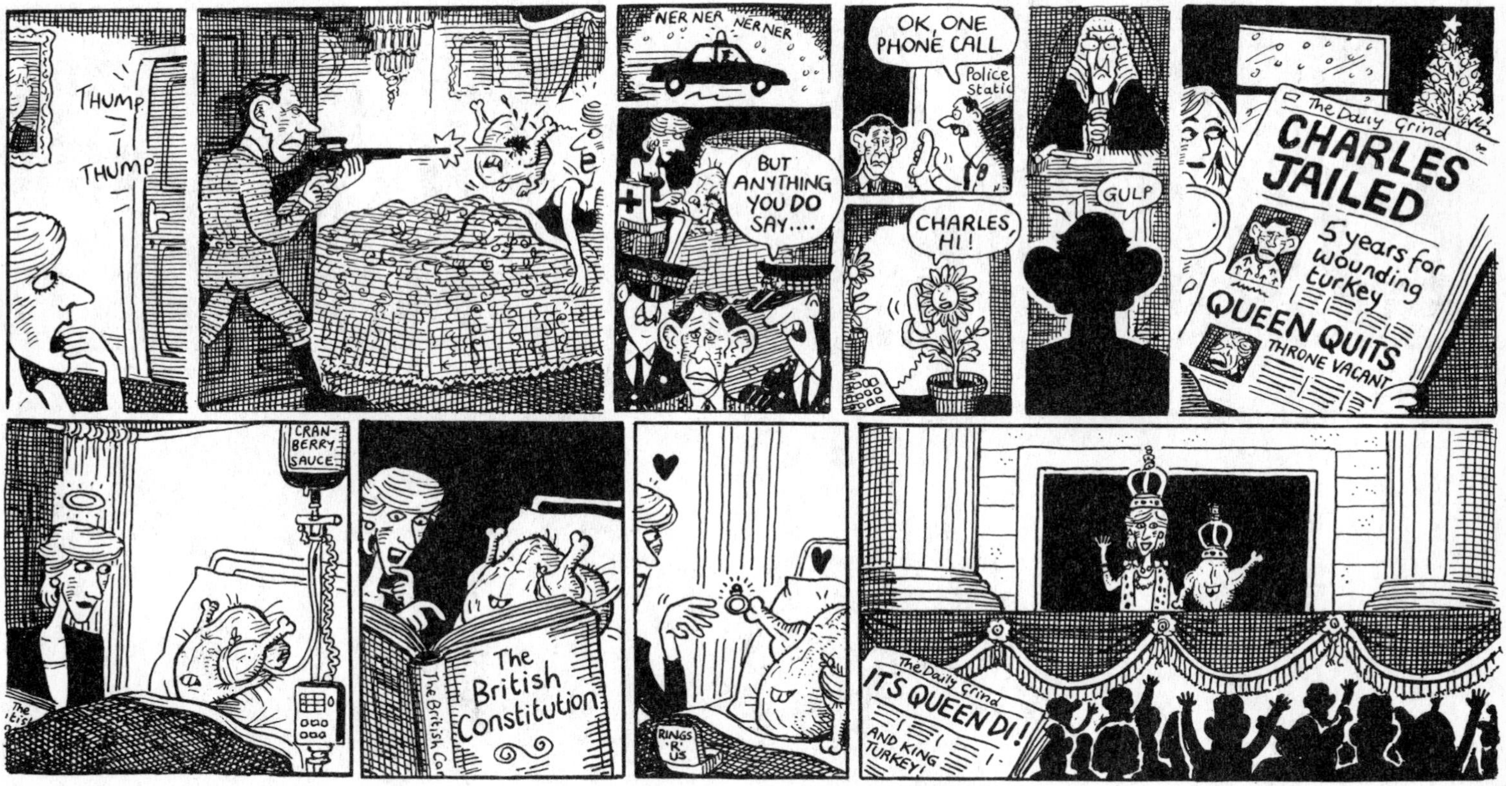
THUMP
THUMP
NER NER NER NER
BUT ANYTHING YOU DO SAY....
OK, ONE PHONE CALL
Police
CHARLES, HI!
GULP
The Daily Grind
CHARLES JAILED
5 years for wounding turkey
QUEEN QUITS
THRONE VACANT
CRAN-BERRY SAUCE
The British Constitution
RINGS 'R' US
The Daily Grind
IT'S QUEEN DI!
AND KING TURKEY!

CONTINUED →

Kipper Williams

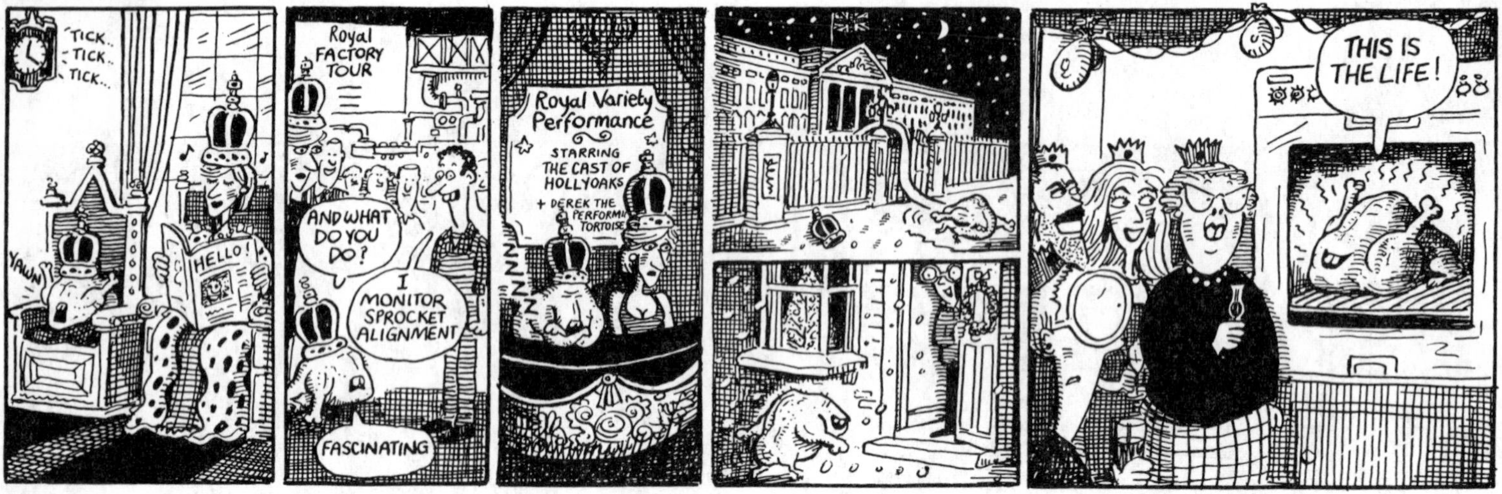
TICK..
TICK..
TICK..
YAWN
HELLO!
Royal FACTORY TOUR
AND WHAT DO YOU DO?
I MONITOR SPROCKET ALIGNMENT
FASCINATING
Royal Variety Performance
STARRING THE CAST OF HOLLYOAKS
+ DEREK THE PERFORMI TORTOISE
ZZZZ
THIS IS THE LIFE!

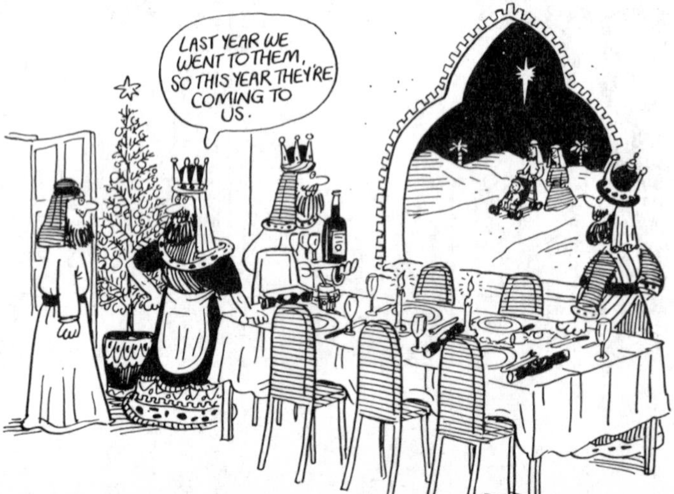
LAST YEAR WE WENT TO THEM, SO THIS YEAR THEY'RE COMING TO US.

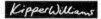

Kipper Williams

IDENTITY PARADE

FLY DRIVE

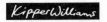

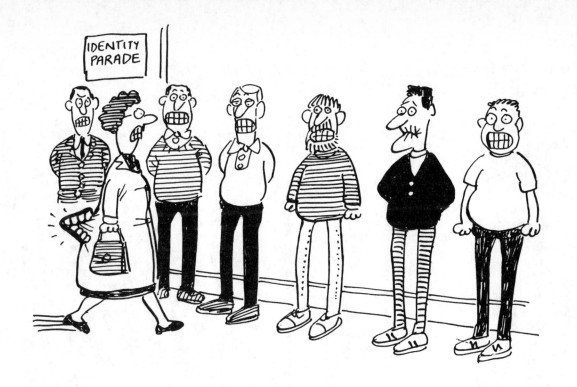

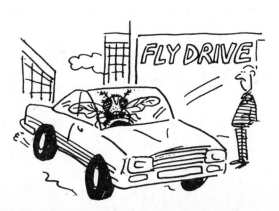

Kipper Williams

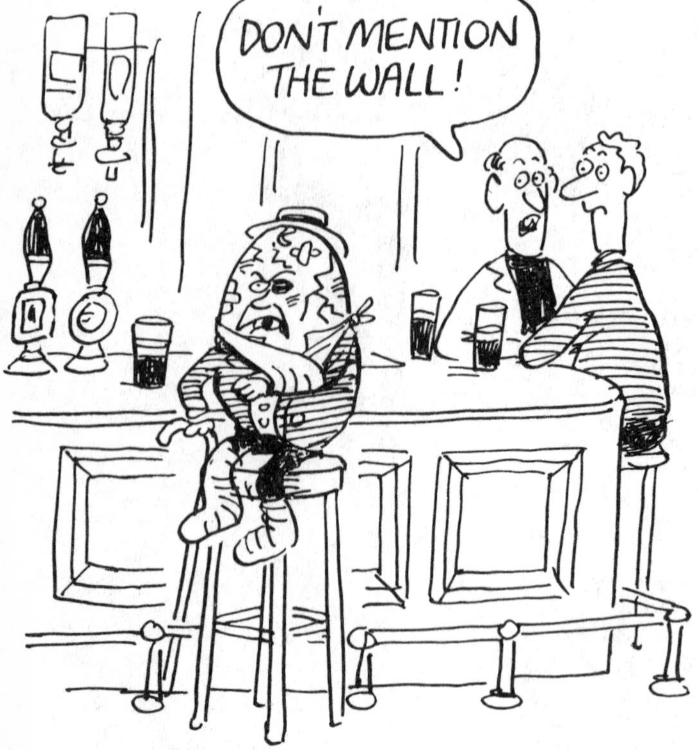
DON'T MENTION THE WALL!

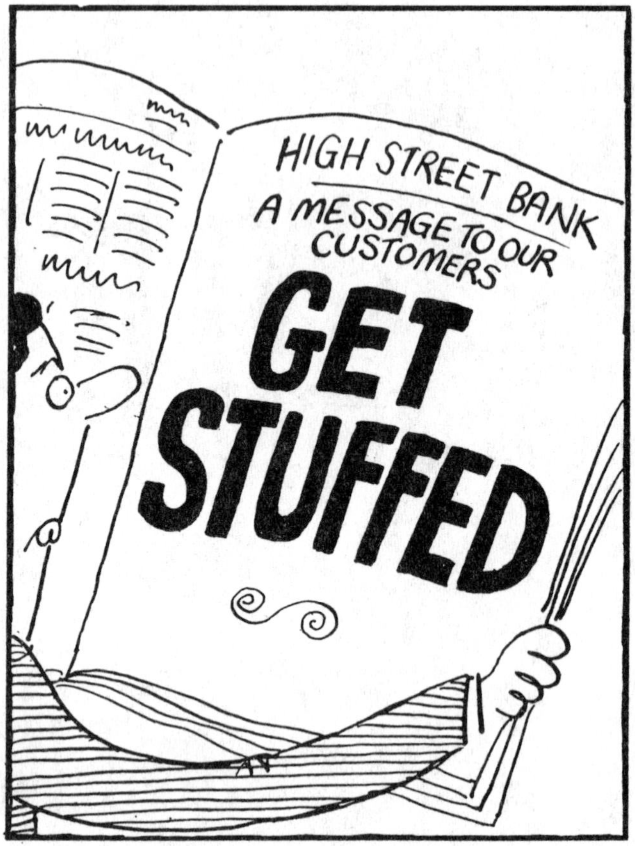
HIGH STREET BANK
A MESSAGE TO OUR CUSTOMERS
GET STUFFED

'I can lick anyone in the house.'

DONUT BAR
I'M DUNKING TO FORGET

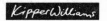

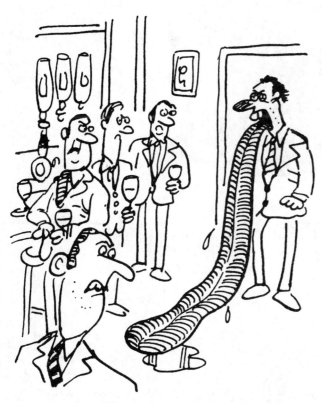

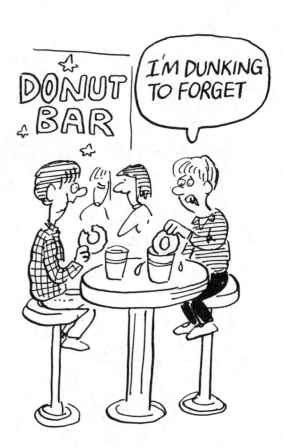

KipperWilliams

WHY AM I DOING THIS?

PILE 'EM HIGH

Someone told me There was a Poetry boom.
Complete Works of QUENTIN FEY
But there Wasn't.
THANKYOU
Complete Works of QUENTIN FEY
ZZZZ
CLAP CLAP

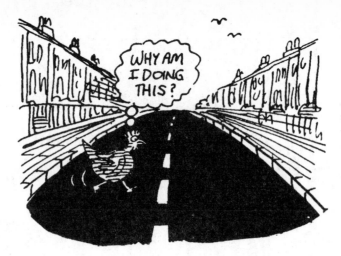

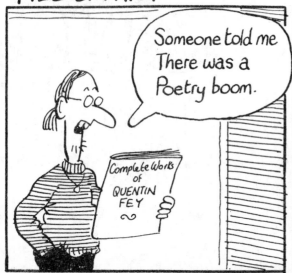

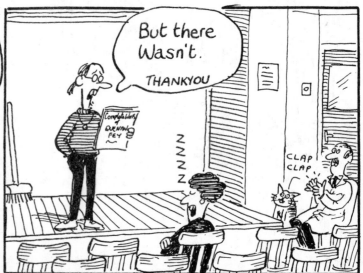

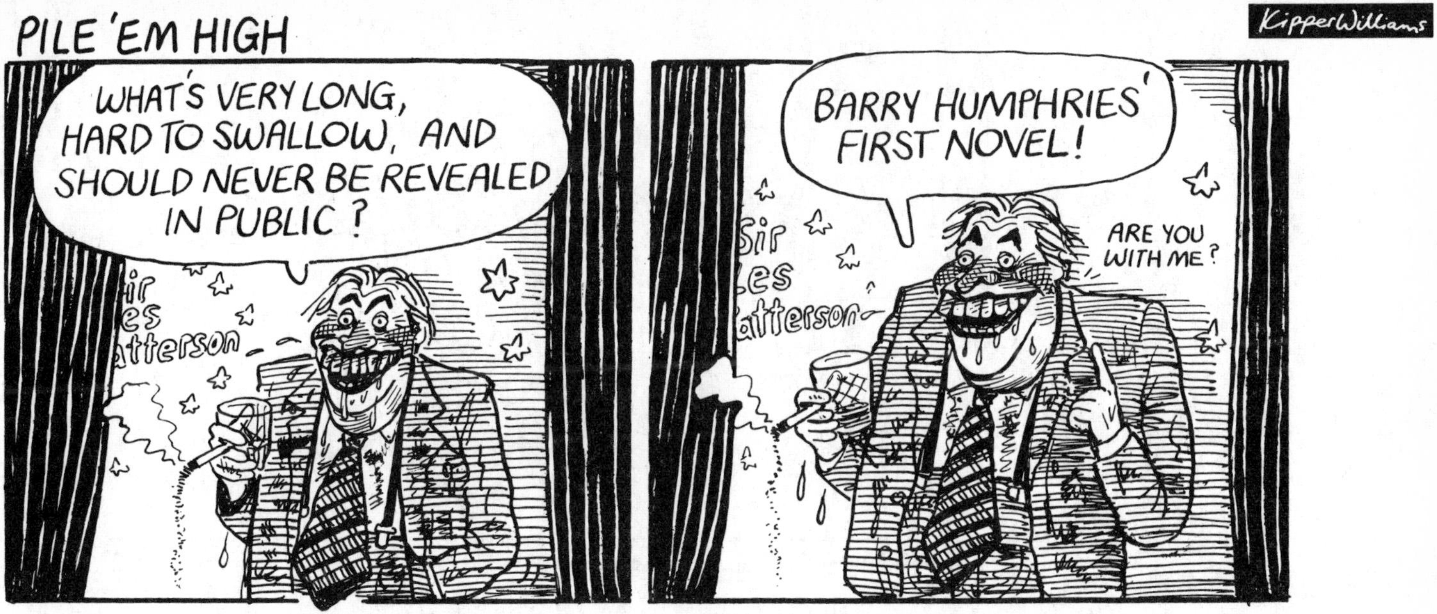
PILE 'EM HIGH
KipperWilliams
WHAT'S VERY LONG, HARD TO SWALLOW, AND SHOULD NEVER BE REVEALED IN PUBLIC?
Sir Les Patterson
BARRY HUMPHRIES' FIRST NOVEL!
ARE YOU WITH ME?

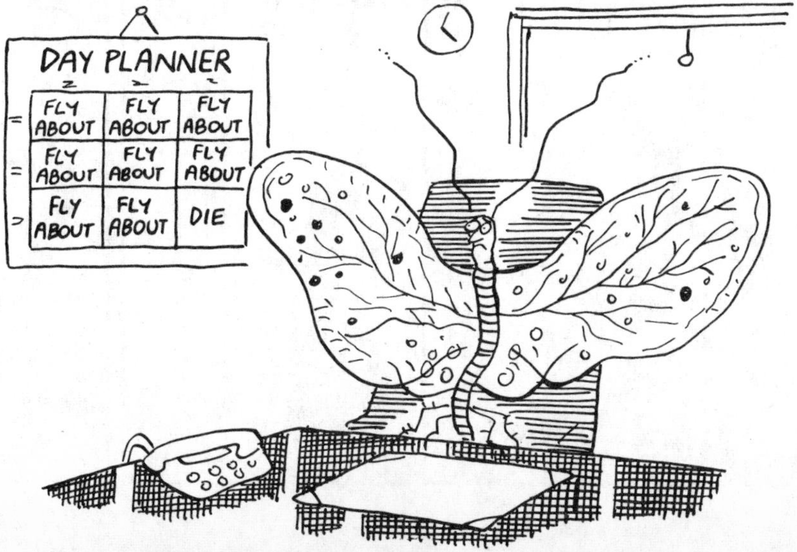
DAY PLANNER
FLY ABOUT
FLY ABOUT
FLY ABOUT
FLY ABOUT
FLY ABOUT
FLY ABOUT
FLY ABOUT
FLY ABOUT
DIE

Kipper Williams

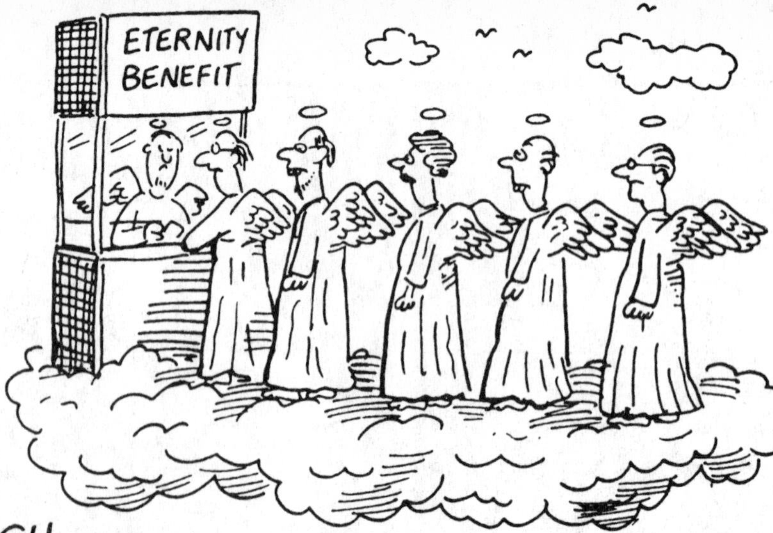

ETERNITY BENEFIT

PILE 'EM HIGH

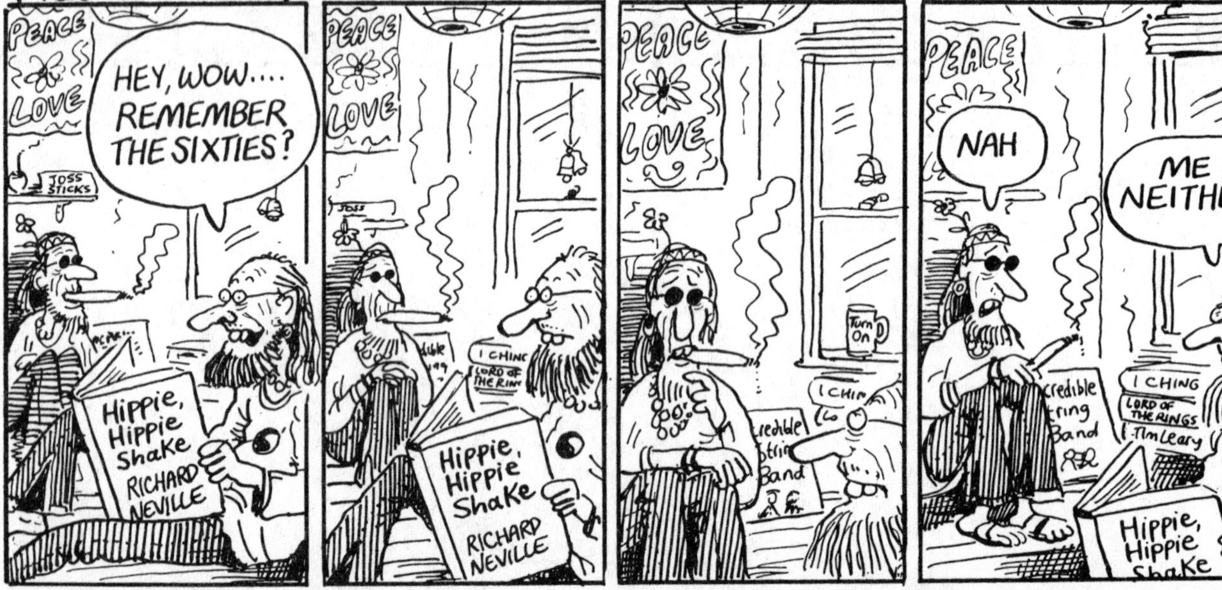

PEACE
LOVE
JOSS STICKS
HEY, WOW.... REMEMBER THE SIXTIES?
Hippie, Hippie Shake
RICHARD NEVILLE
I CHING
LORD OF THE RINGS
Turn On
NAH
ME NEITHER
Tim Leary

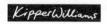

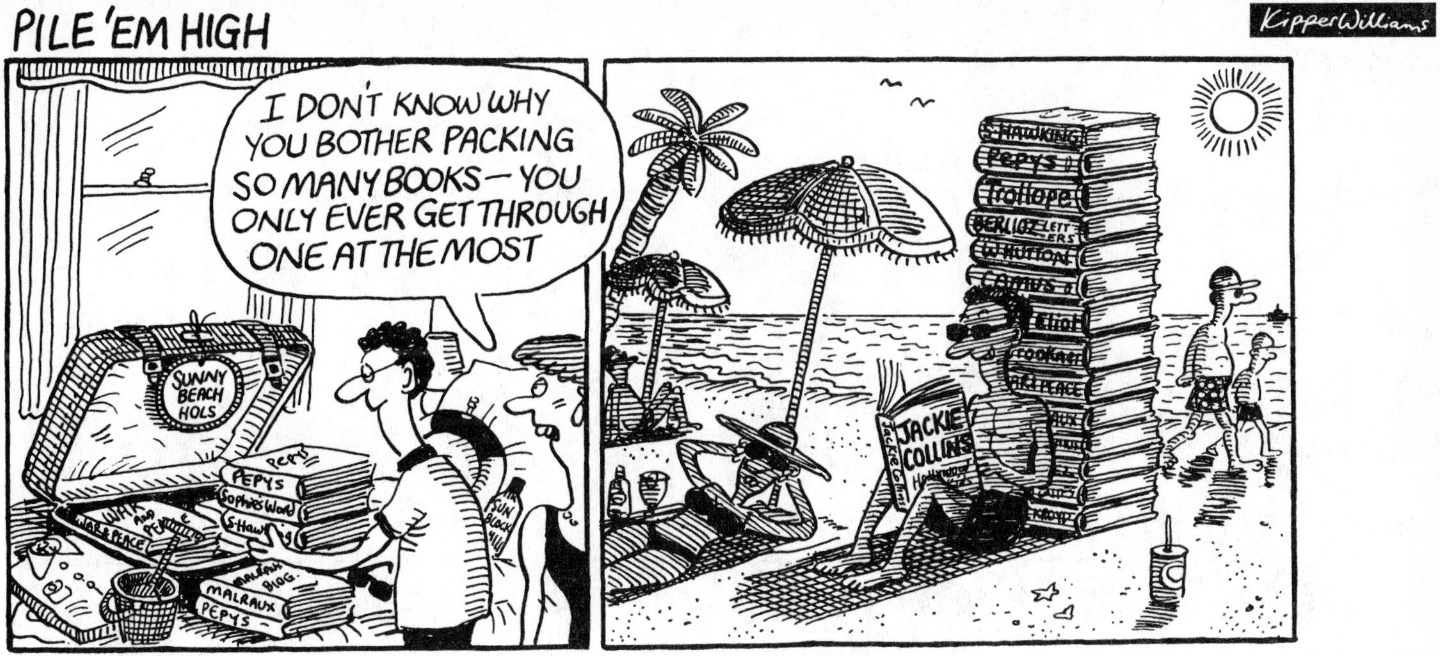
PILE 'EM HIGH
Kipper Williams
I DON'T KNOW WHY YOU BOTHER PACKING SO MANY BOOKS — YOU ONLY EVER GET THROUGH ONE AT THE MOST
SUNNY BEACH HOLS
PEPYS
PEPYS
Sophie's World
MALRAUX BIOG.
MALRAUX
PEPYS
SUN BLOCK
S-HAWKING
Pepys
Trollope
BERLIOZ LETTERS
W HUTTON
CAMUS
Eliot
JACKIE COLLINS

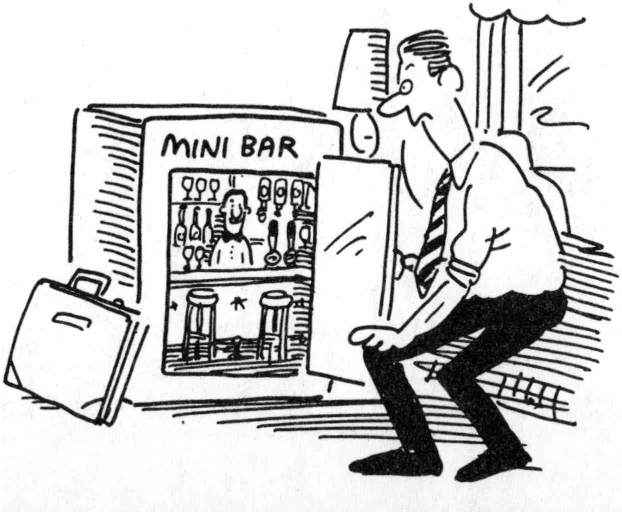
MINI BAR

Kipper Williams

'I know where you live.'

PILE 'EM HIGH

NOT THAT I'VE ACTUALLY READ IT
A BRIEF HISTORY OF TIME
Stephen Hawking
MEAN-WHILE, IN A PARALLEL UNIVERSE ....
NOT THAT I'VE ACTUALLY READ IT
BLACK HOLES AND BABY UNIVERSES
Stephen Hawking

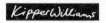

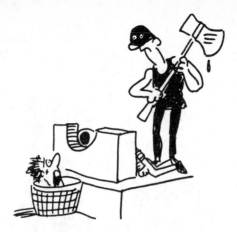

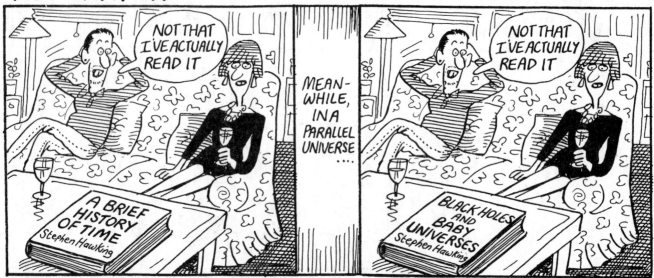

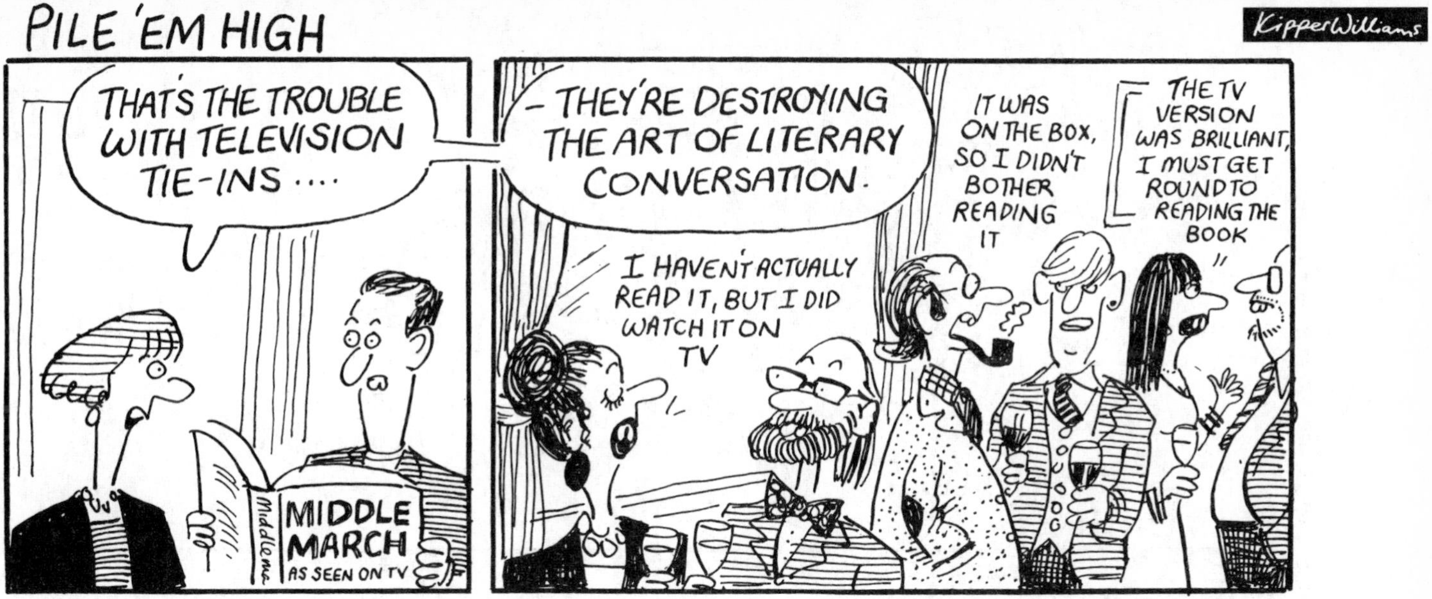
PILE 'EM HIGH
Kipper Williams
THAT'S THE TROUBLE WITH TELEVISION TIE-INS ....
– THEY'RE DESTROYING THE ART OF LITERARY CONVERSATION.
MIDDLE MARCH
AS SEEN ON TV
Middlemarch
I HAVEN'T ACTUALLY READ IT, BUT I DID WATCH IT ON TV
IT WAS ON THE BOX, SO I DIDN'T BOTHER READING IT
THE TV VERSION WAS BRILLIANT, I MUST GET ROUND TO READING THE BOOK

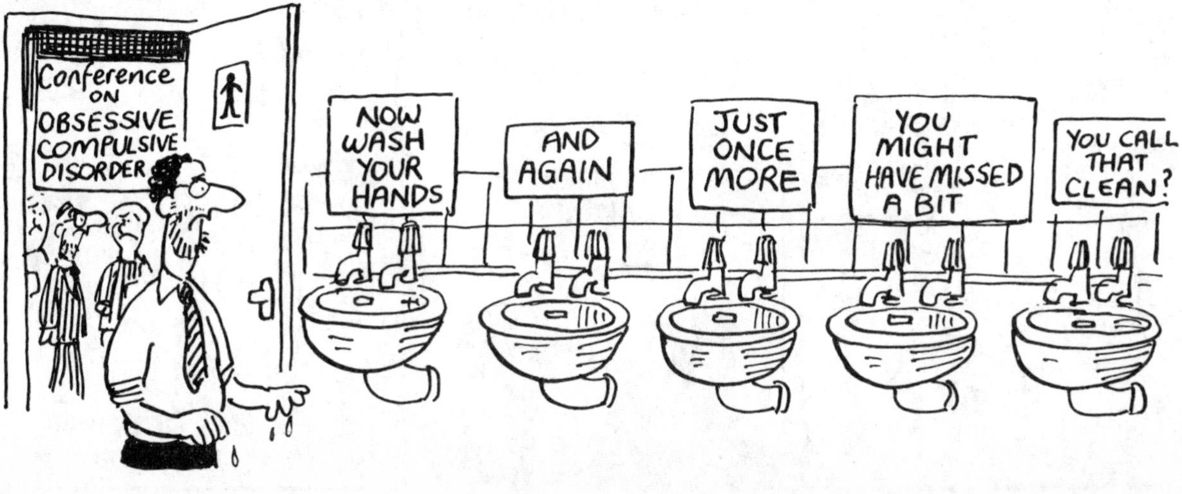
Conference ON OBSESSIVE COMPULSIVE DISORDER
NOW WASH YOUR HANDS
AND AGAIN
JUST ONCE MORE
YOU MIGHT HAVE MISSED A BIT
YOU CALL THAT CLEAN?

Kipper Williams

RAMBLERS DEMAND RIGHT OF WAY

PILE 'EM HIGH

THERE ISN'T MUCH SCANDAL HERE
PRINCE EDWARD BIOGRAPHY
Prince Edward
HE DOESN'T SUFFER FROM BULIMIA, HE ISN'T SEPARATED, HE DOESN'T KEEP PUTTING HIS FOOT IN IT....
SO HE CAN'T BE A GENUINE ROYAL!
SCANDAL!
PRINCE EDWARD BIOGRAPHY
PRINCE

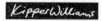

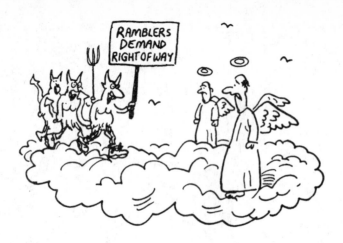

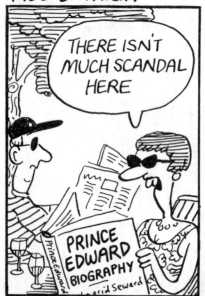

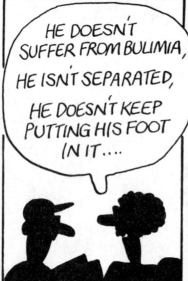

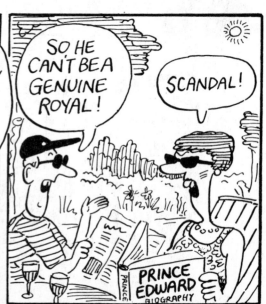

PILE 'EM HIGH

Kipper Williams

THOSE ROYAL BOOKS SHOULDN'T BE ON DISPLAY LIKE THAT...
-THEY OUGHT TO BE SEPARATED
WHAT ABOUT THE CHILDREN?
BIOGRAPHY
DIANA Her True Story
CHARLES
Diana Her New Life
PRINCE OF WALES
Princess in Love
DIANA Her Life in Photos
Prince of Wales
Prince Harry

WE'VE TIED THE KANGAROO DOWN, SPORT
ZOO WATCH LIVE with Rolf Harris

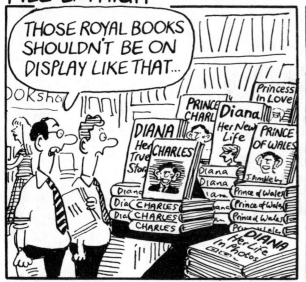

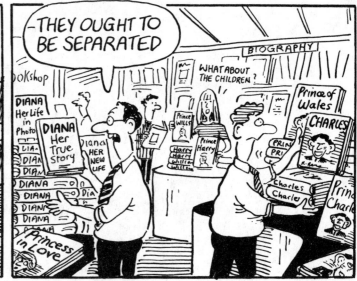

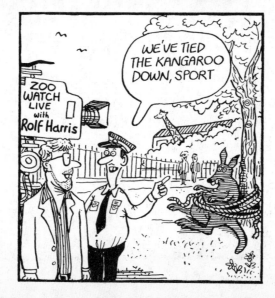

KipperWilliams

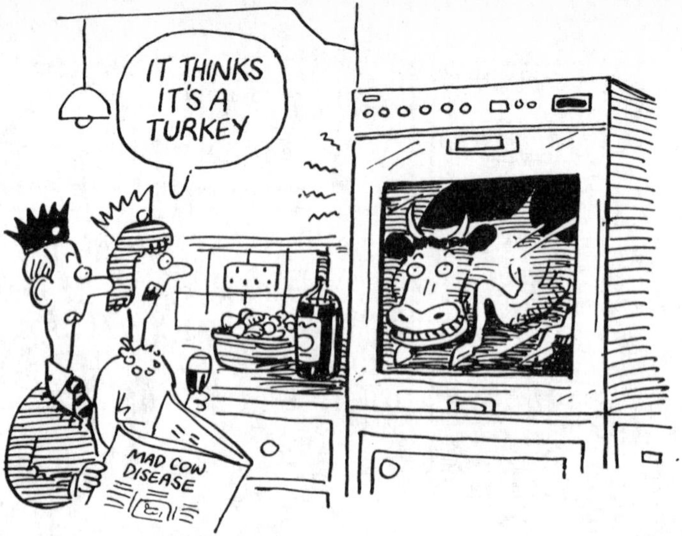
IT THINKS IT'S A TURKEY
MAD COW DISEASE

PILE 'EM HIGH

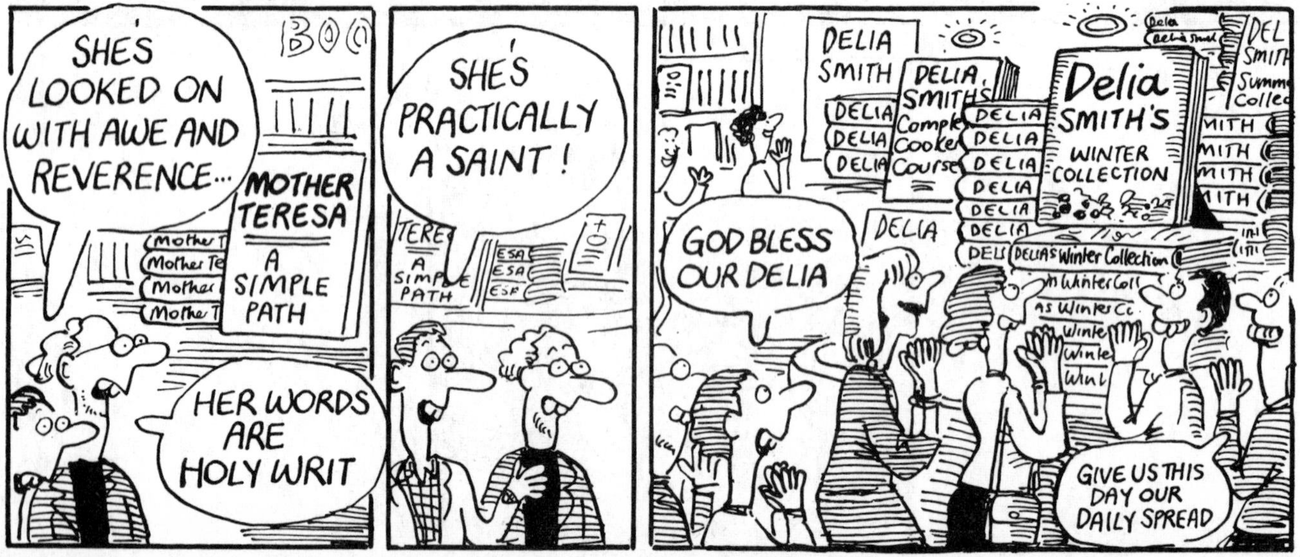
SHE'S LOOKED ON WITH AWE AND REVERENCE...
MOTHER TERESA
A SIMPLE PATH
HER WORDS ARE HOLY WRIT
SHE'S PRACTICALLY A SAINT!
DELIA SMITH
DELIA SMITH'S Complete Cookery Course
Delia SMITH'S WINTER COLLECTION
DELIAS Winter Collection
GOD BLESS OUR DELIA
GIVE US THIS DAY OUR DAILY SPREAD

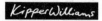

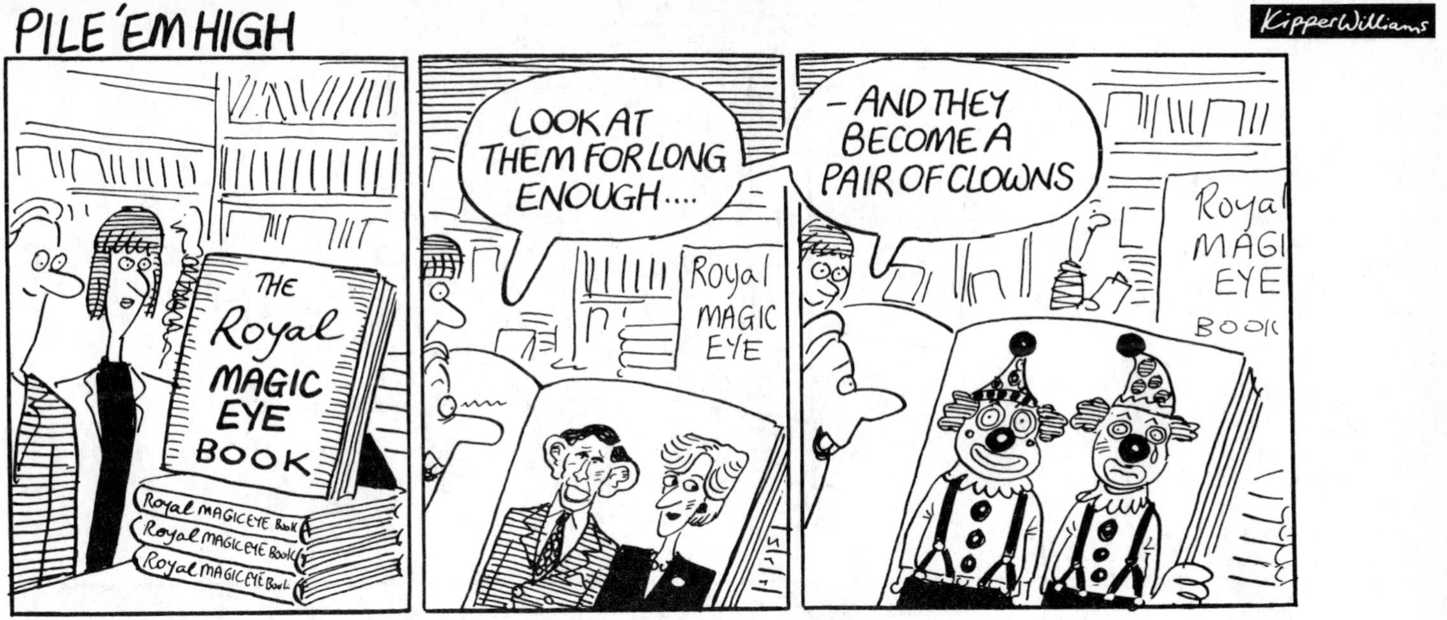
PILE 'EM HIGH
KipperWilliams
THE Royal MAGIC EYE BOOK
Royal MAGIC EYE Book
Royal MAGIC EYE Book
Royal MAGIC EYE Book
LOOK AT THEM FOR LONG ENOUGH....
Royal MAGIC EYE
- AND THEY BECOME A PAIR OF CLOWNS
Royal MAGI EYE BOOK

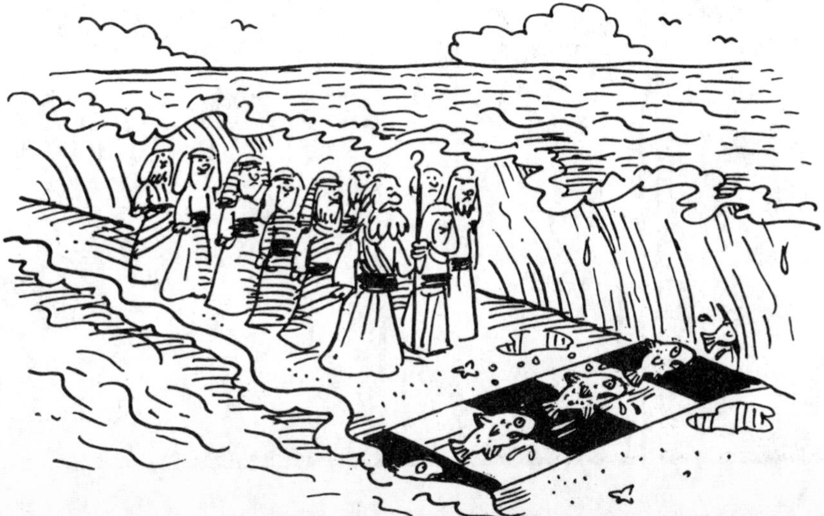

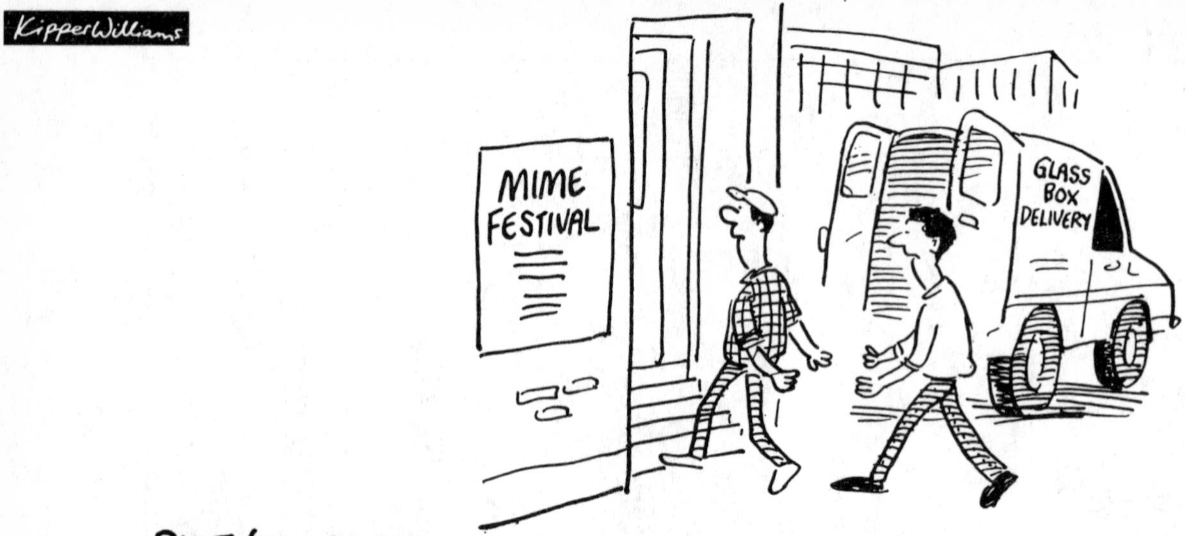
KipperWilliams
MIME FESTIVAL
GLASS BOX DELIVERY

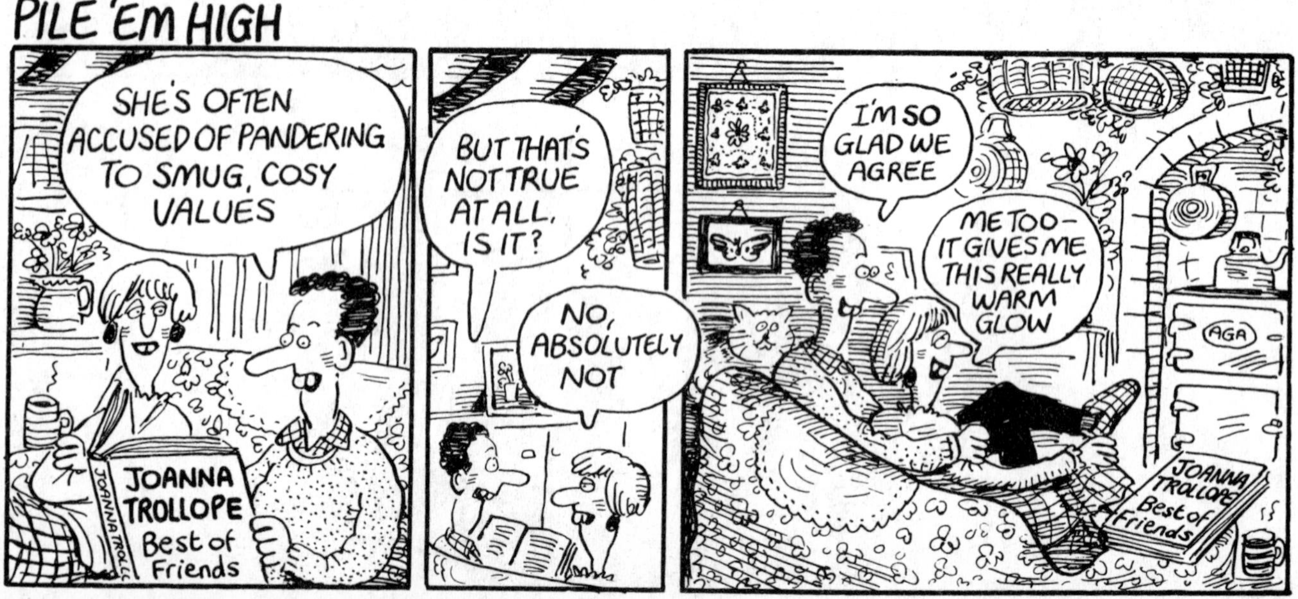
PILE 'EM HIGH
SHE'S OFTEN ACCUSED OF PANDERING TO SMUG, COSY VALUES
JOANNA TROLLOPE Best of Friends
BUT THAT'S NOT TRUE AT ALL, IS IT?
NO, ABSOLUTELY NOT
I'M SO GLAD WE AGREE
ME TOO- IT GIVES ME THIS REALLY WARM GLOW
AGA
JOANNA TROLLOPE Best of Friends

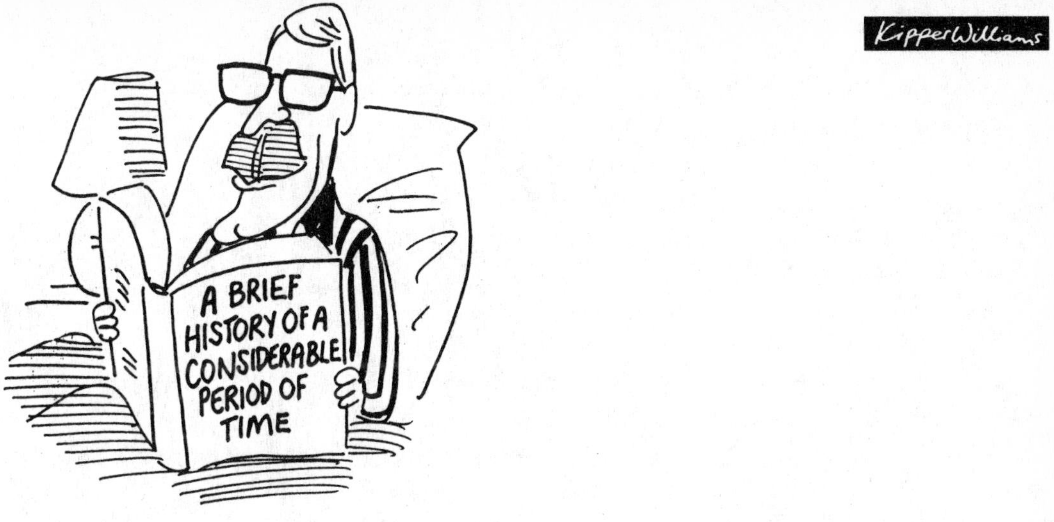
A BRIEF HISTORY OF A CONSIDERABLE PERIOD OF TIME
KipperWilliams

PILE 'EM HIGH

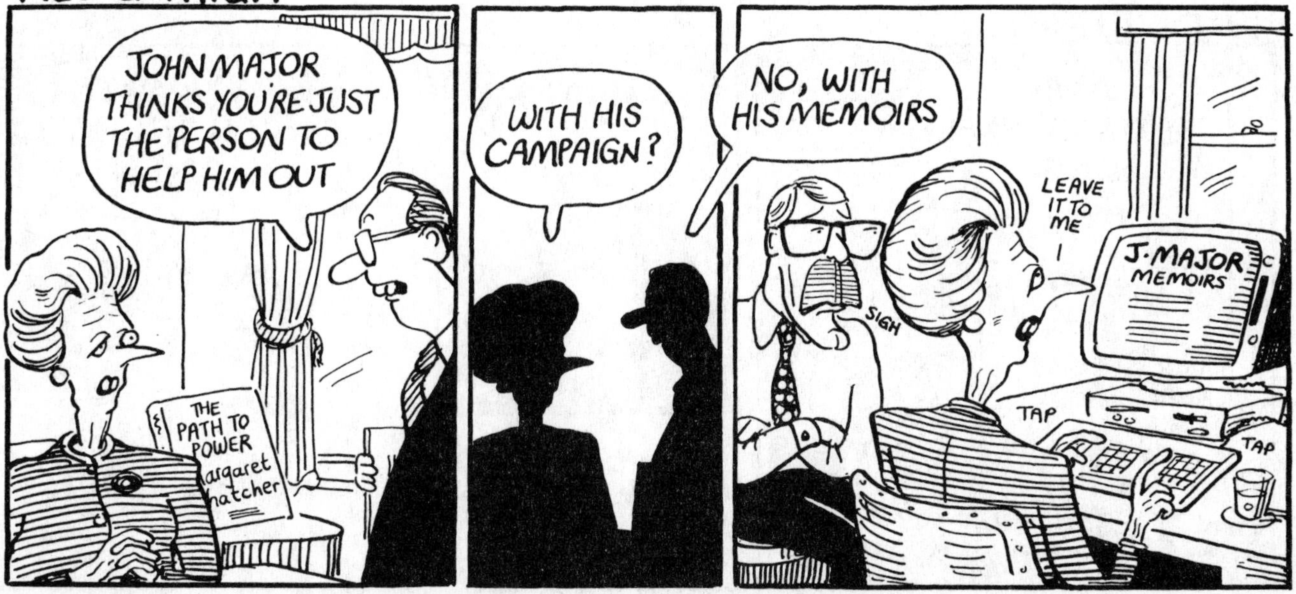
JOHN MAJOR THINKS YOU'RE JUST THE PERSON TO HELP HIM OUT
THE PATH TO POWER
argaret
hatcher
WITH HIS CAMPAIGN?
NO, WITH HIS MEMOIRS
SIGH
LEAVE IT TO ME
J. MAJOR MEMOIRS
TAP
TAP

Kipper Williams

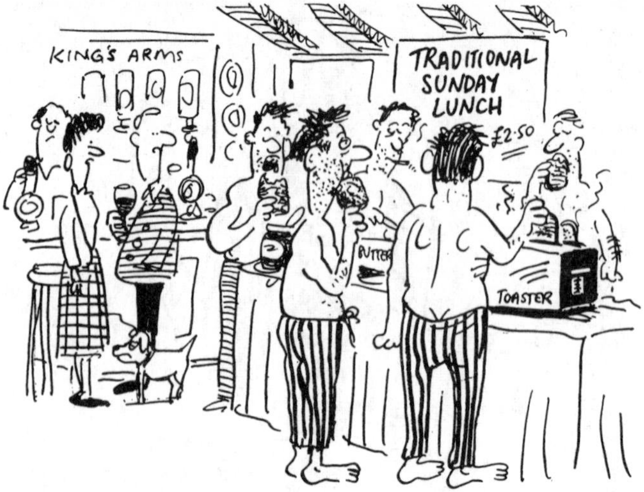
KING'S ARMS
TRADITIONAL SUNDAY LUNCH
£2·50
BUTTER
TOASTER

PILE 'EM HIGH

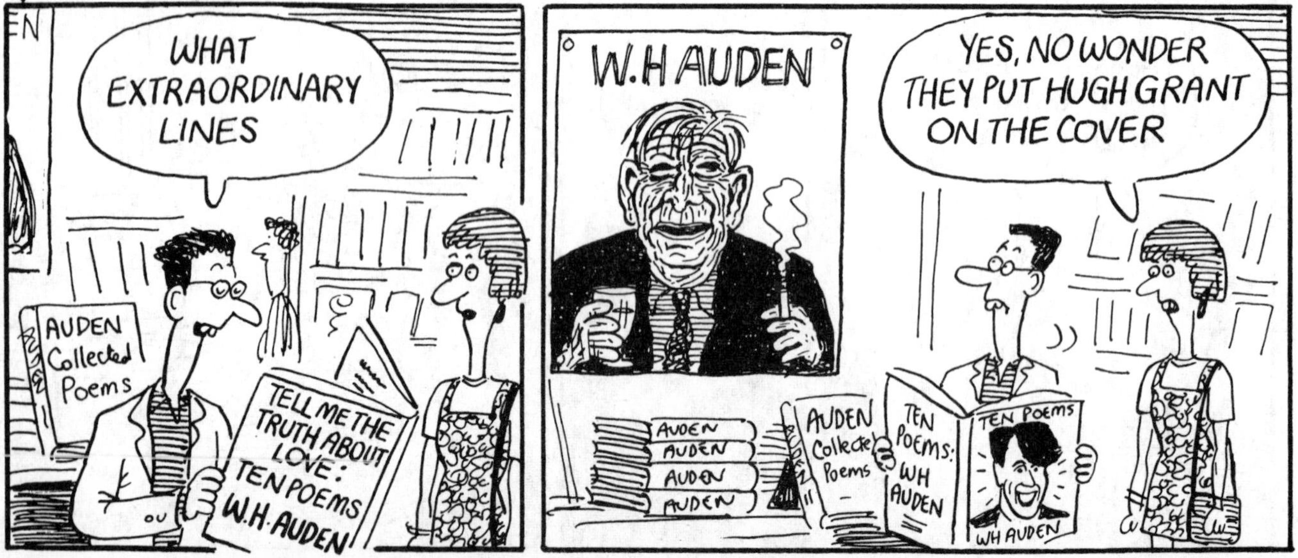
WHAT EXTRAORDINARY LINES
AUDEN Collected Poems
TELL ME THE TRUTH ABOUT LOVE: TEN POEMS W.H. AUDEN
W.H AUDEN
YES, NO WONDER THEY PUT HUGH GRANT ON THE COVER
AUDEN
AUDEN
AUDEN
AUDEN
AUDEN Collected Poems
TEN POEMS: WH AUDEN
TEN POEMS
WH AUDEN

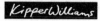

PILE 'EM HIGH

Kipper Williams

LOAD OF NONSENSE
ENTRICS
I'M A LITTLE TEAPOT
I ♥ ARSENAL
?
ECCENT-RICS
IT'LL NEVER SELL
Eccentrics
BEST CUSTARD
BOOKS
CRAZY IDEA FOR A BOOK
ECCENTRICS
ECCEN
ECCEN
ECCEN
ENTRICS
ENTRICS
ENTRICS
ENTRICS
CENTRICS
GIVE ME WILLIAM McGONAGALL ANYDAY

IF IT ISN'T KILLER WHALES IT'S DAVID ATTENBOROUGH
TRIALS OF LIFE

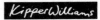

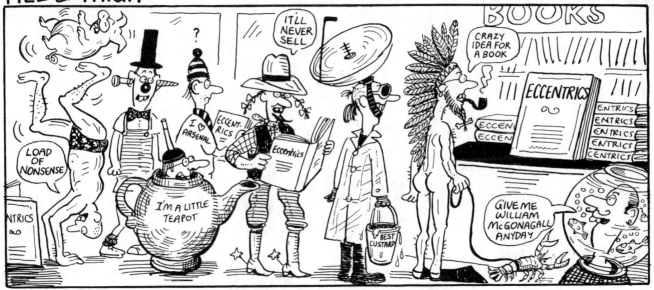

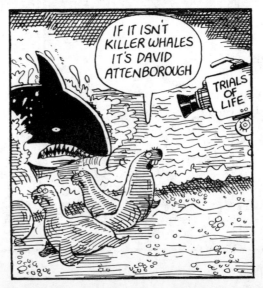

Kipper Williams

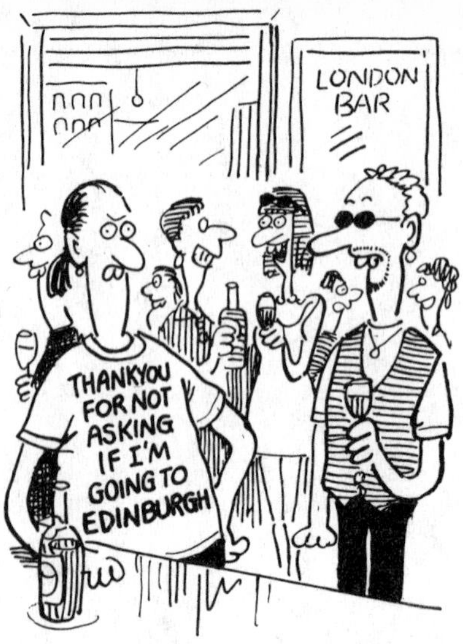
LONDON BAR
THANKYOU FOR NOT ASKING IF I'M GOING TO EDINBURGH

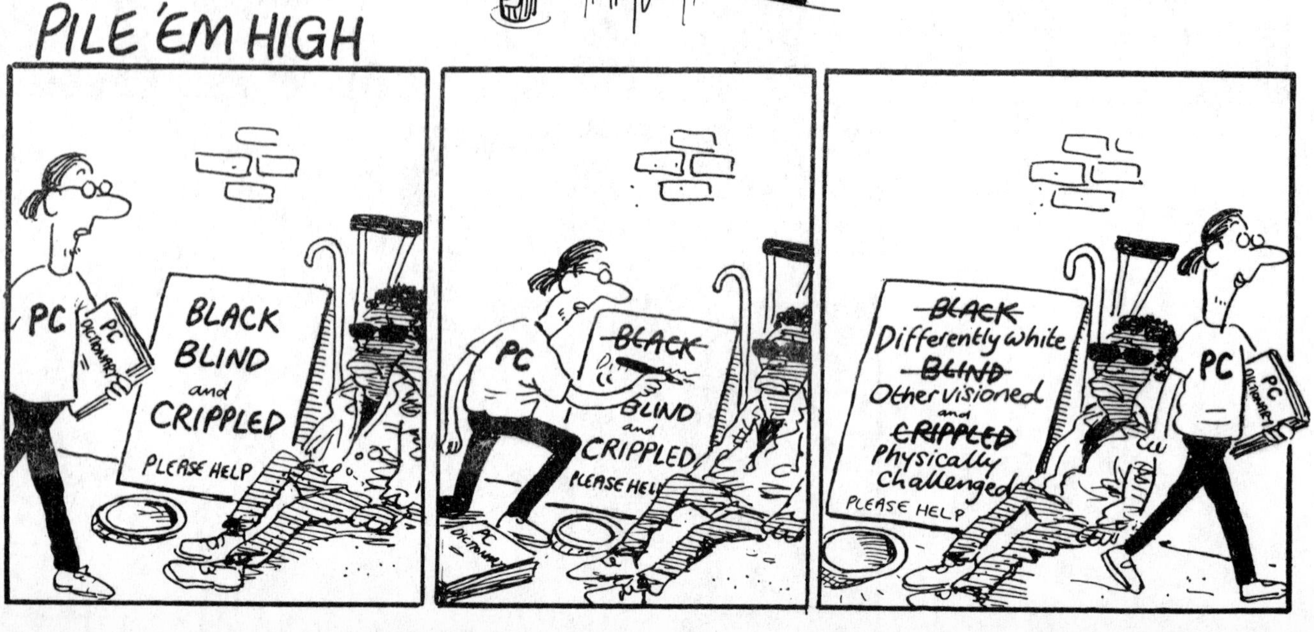
PILE 'EM HIGH
PC
PC DICTIONARY
BLACK
BLIND
and
CRIPPLED
PLEASE HELP
PC
~~BLACK~~
BLIND
and
CRIPPLED
PC DICTIONARY
~~BLACK~~
Differently white
~~BLIND~~
Other visioned
and
~~CRIPPLED~~
Physically Challenged
PLEASE HELP
PC
PC DICTIONARY

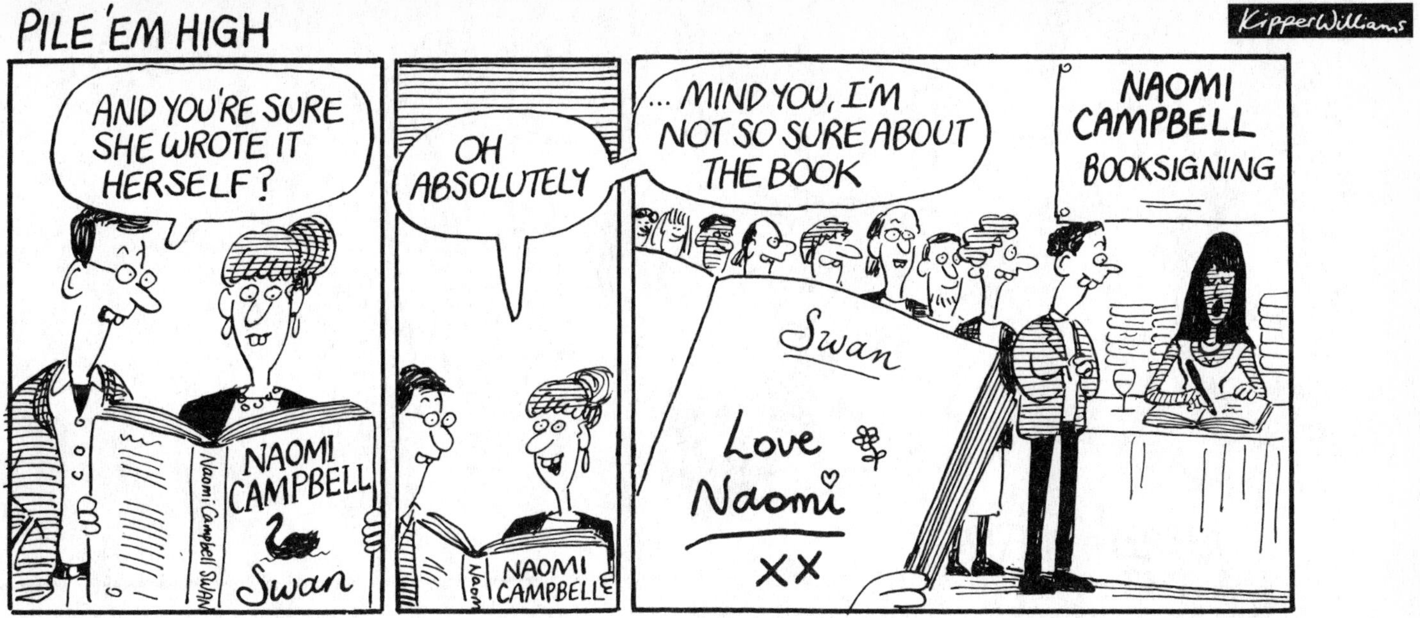
PILE 'EM HIGH
KipperWilliams
AND YOU'RE SURE SHE WROTE IT HERSELF?
NAOMI CAMPBELL
Naomi Campbell SWAN
Swan
OH ABSOLUTELY
NAOMI CAMPBELL
... MIND YOU, I'M NOT SO SURE ABOUT THE BOOK
NAOMI CAMPBELL BOOKSIGNING
Swan
Love Naomi
XX

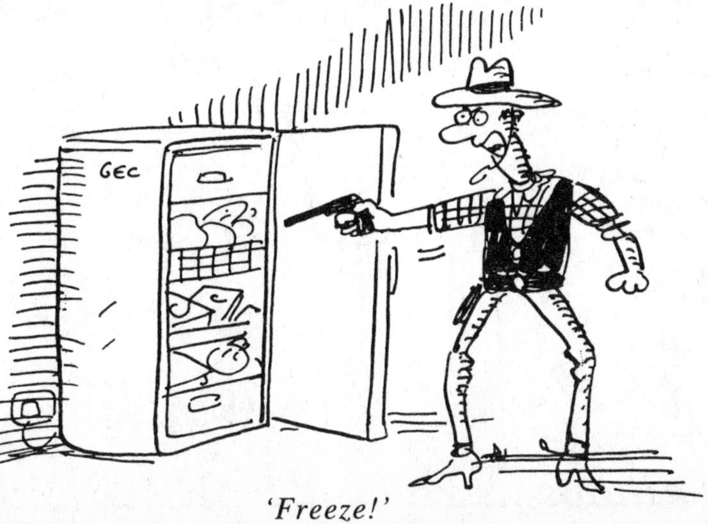
GEC

'Freeze!'

KipperWilliams

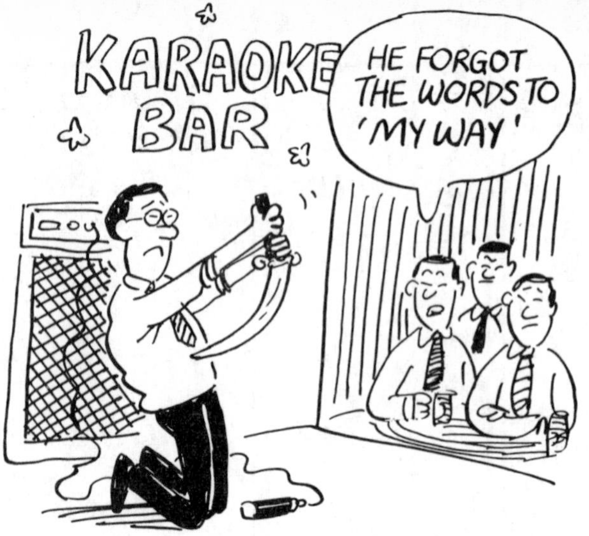
KARAOKE BAR
HE FORGOT THE WORDS TO 'MY WAY'

PILE 'EM HIGH

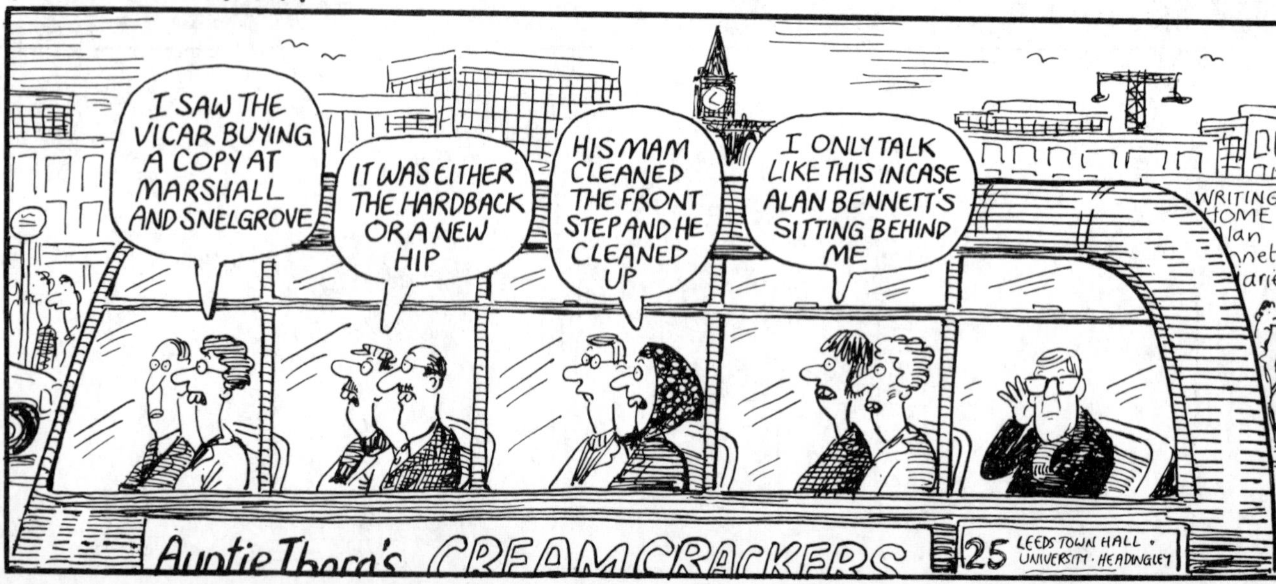
I SAW THE VICAR BUYING A COPY AT MARSHALL AND SNELGROVE
IT WAS EITHER THE HARDBACK OR A NEW HIP
HIS MAM CLEANED THE FRONT STEP AND HE CLEANED UP
I ONLY TALK LIKE THIS IN CASE ALAN BENNETT'S SITTING BEHIND ME
WRITING
HOME
Auntie Thora's CREAM CRACKERS
25 LEEDS TOWN HALL • UNIVERSITY • HEADINGLEY

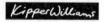

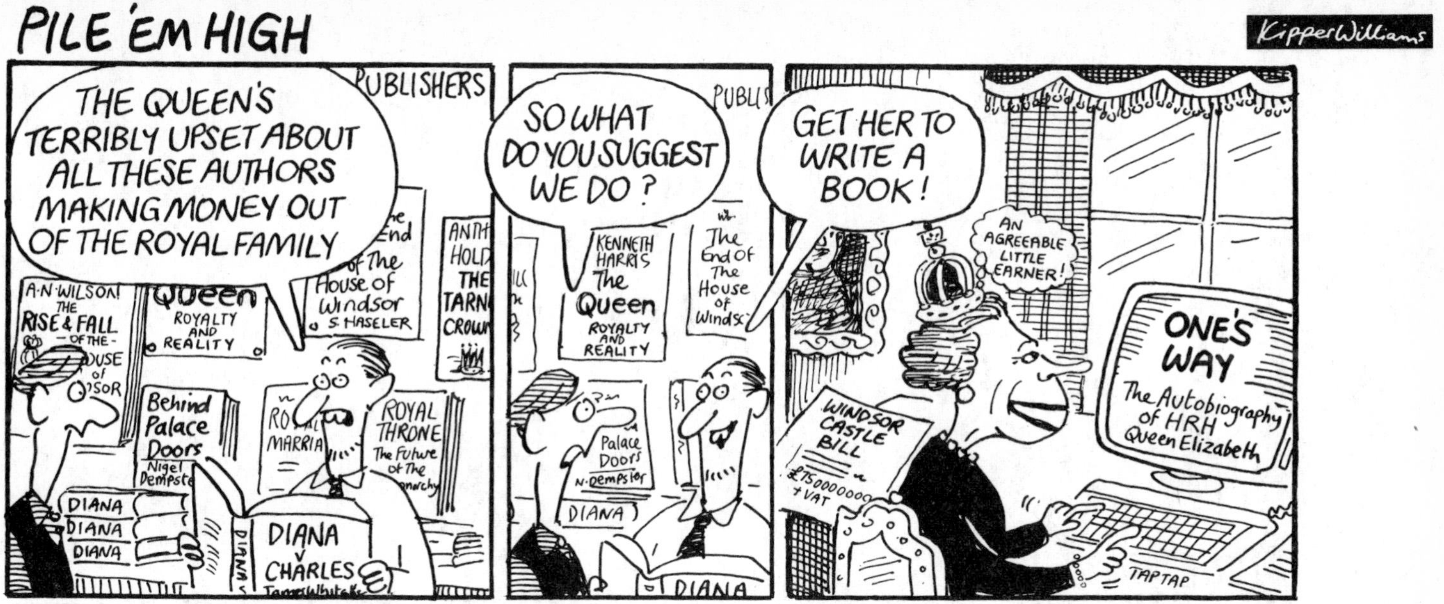
PILE 'EM HIGH
KipperWilliams
PUBLISHERS
THE QUEEN'S TERRIBLY UPSET ABOUT ALL THESE AUTHORS MAKING MONEY OUT OF THE ROYAL FAMILY
A·N·WILSON! THE RISE & FALL OF THE HOUSE of WINDSOR
Queen ROYALTY AND REALITY
The End of The House of Windsor S. HASELER
Behind Palace Doors Nigel Dempster
ROYAL THRONE The Future of The Monarchy
DIANA
DIANA
DIANA
DIANA v CHARLES
SO WHAT DO YOU SUGGEST WE DO?
KENNETH HARRIS The Queen ROYALTY AND REALITY
The End Of The House of Windsor
Palace Doors N. Dempster
DIANA
DIANA
GET HER TO WRITE A BOOK!
AN AGREEABLE LITTLE EARNER!
WINDSOR CASTLE BILL £750000000 + VAT
ONE'S WAY
The Autobiography of HRH Queen Elizabeth
TAPTAP

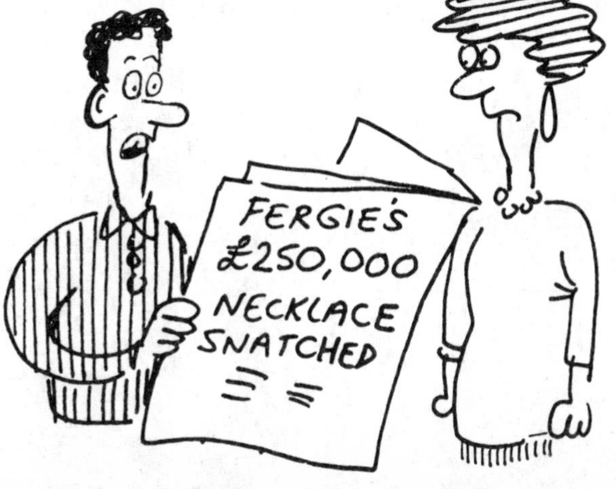
FERGIE'S £250,000 NECKLACE SNATCHED

'The £250,000 had sentimental value.'

KipperWilliams

DWARFARIN

PILE 'EM HIGH

ACME PUBLISHING
THE QUEEN!
Elizabeth
ELIZABETH II
THE MONARCHY
BEHIND PALACE DOORS
ANA
Charles
Princess in Love
ROYAL BOOK SALES
ROYAL REVELATIONS
MORE ROYAL SCANDAL
PALACE GOSSIP
"PHILIP'S INFIDELITY"

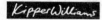

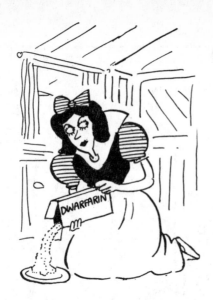

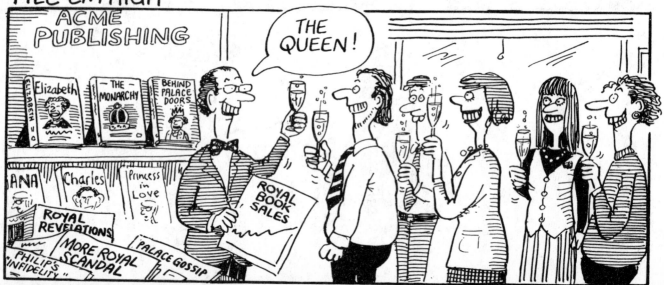

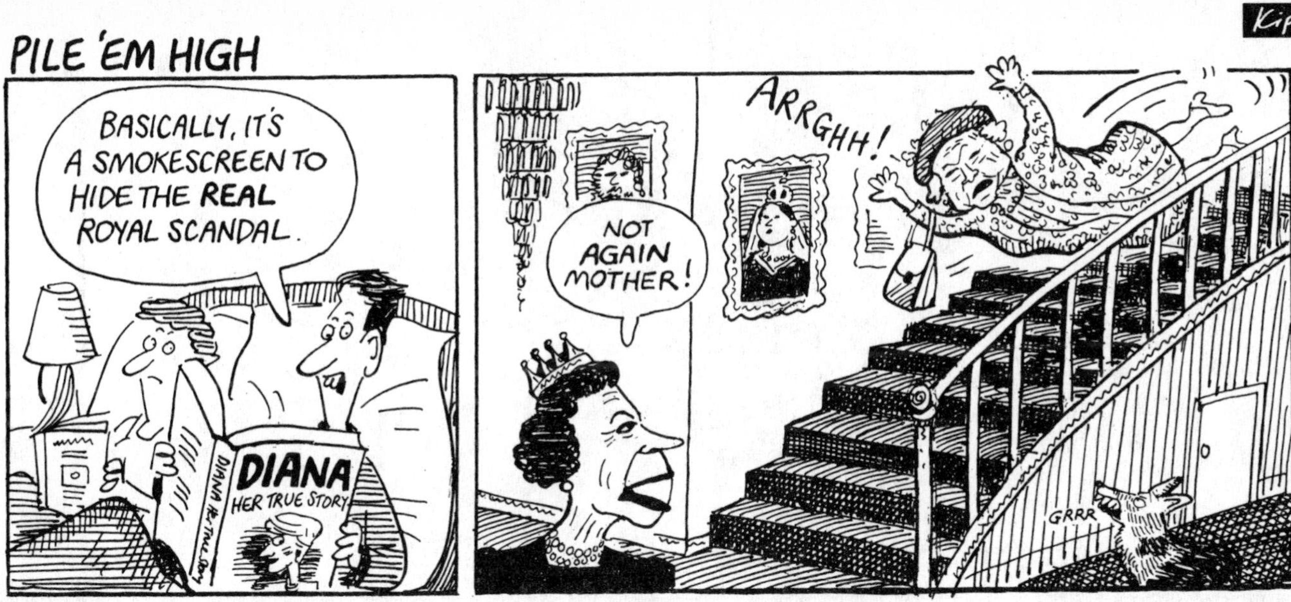
Kipper Williams
PILE 'EM HIGH
BASICALLY, IT'S A SMOKESCREEN TO HIDE THE REAL ROYAL SCANDAL.
DIANA
HER TRUE STORY
DIANA HER TRUE STORY
NOT AGAIN MOTHER!
ARRGHH!
GRRR

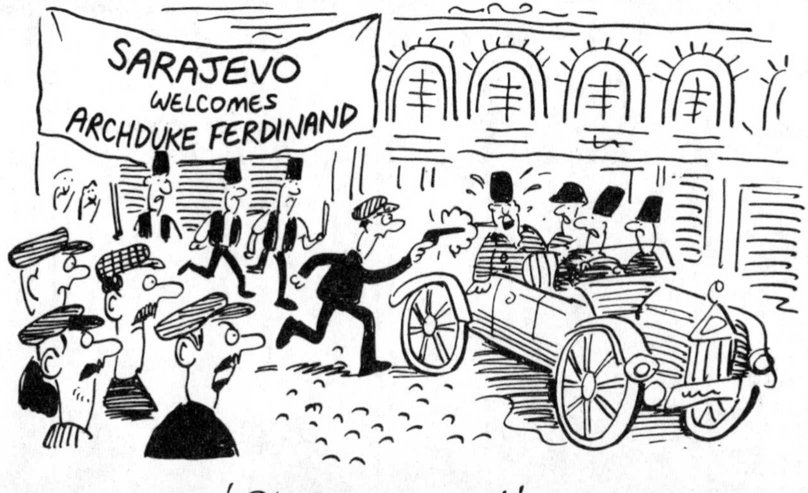
SARAJEVO
WELCOMES
ARCHDUKE FERDINAND

'Bloody students!'

'Lunch is for wimps.'

PILE 'EM HIGH

Six years ago I wrote a book, It had a go at men,

WENDY COPE POETRY READING

SERIOUS CONCERNS

My publisher said 'Wendy— Why not slag them off again?'

SERIOUS CONCERNS

The trouble is with bloody men, They're liars, cheats and crooks,

SERIOUS CONCERNS

But how am I to hate them, When they buy my bloody books?

COME BACK PAM AYRES!

SERIOUS CON

PILE 'EM HIGH

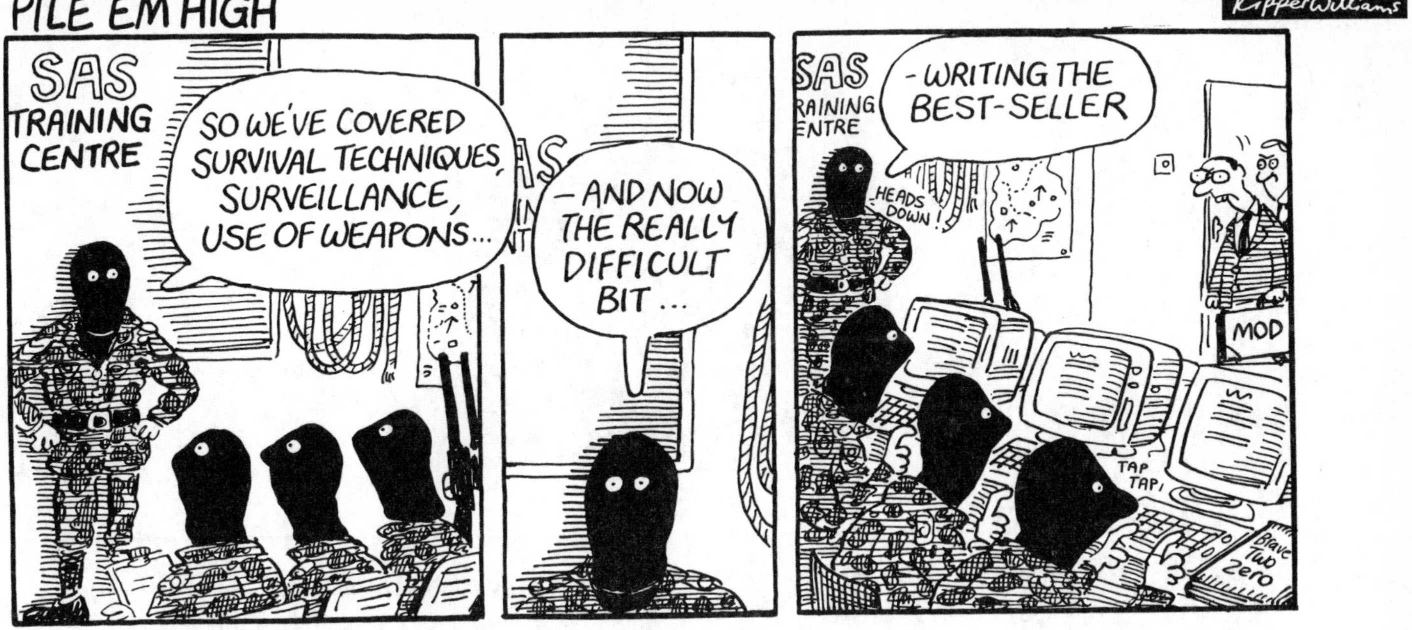

Kipper Williams
SAS TRAINING CENTRE
SO WE'VE COVERED SURVIVAL TECHNIQUES, SURVEILLANCE, USE OF WEAPONS...
– AND NOW THE REALLY DIFFICULT BIT ...
– WRITING THE BEST-SELLER
HEADS DOWN!
MOD
TAP TAP!
Brave Two Zero

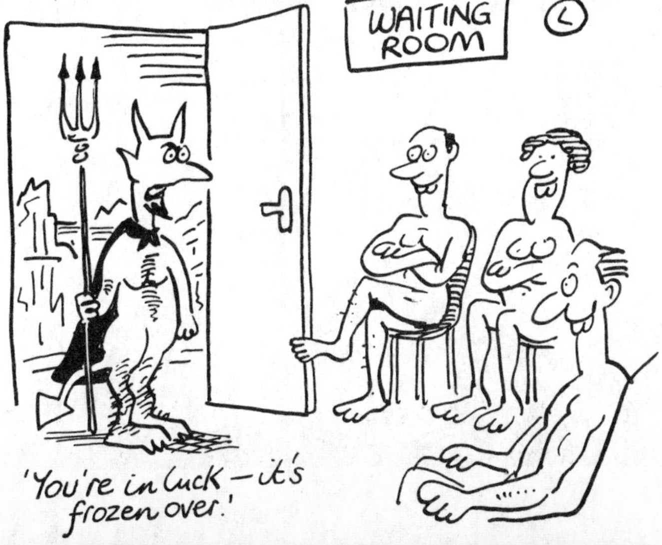

WAITING ROOM

'You're in luck – it's frozen over.'

HUMBLE POTATOES
NOBLE CARROTS
SIMPLE PARSNIPS
MUCH-MALIGNED CABBAGES

PILE 'EM HIGH

IT'S ALL RATHER SHOCKING — ONE SIMPLY DOESN'T ASSOCIATE JEFFREY ARCHER WITH THAT SORT OF THING
Jeffrey Archer BIOGRAPHY by Michael Crick
STRANGER THAN FICTION
HOW DO YOU MEAN?
IT'S ABSOLUTELY FASCINATING, EMINENTLY READABLE, AND I WAS GRIPPED FROM START TO FINISH
Jeffrey Archer BIOGRAPHY
HE MUST HAVE REFUSED TO CO-OPERATE

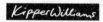

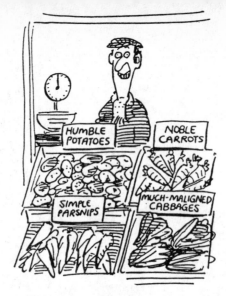

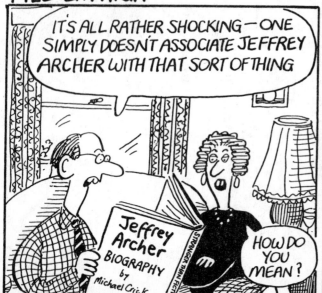

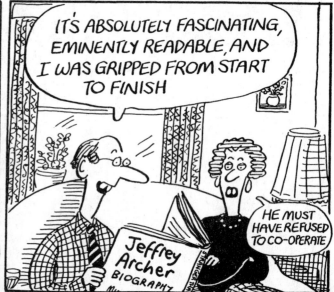

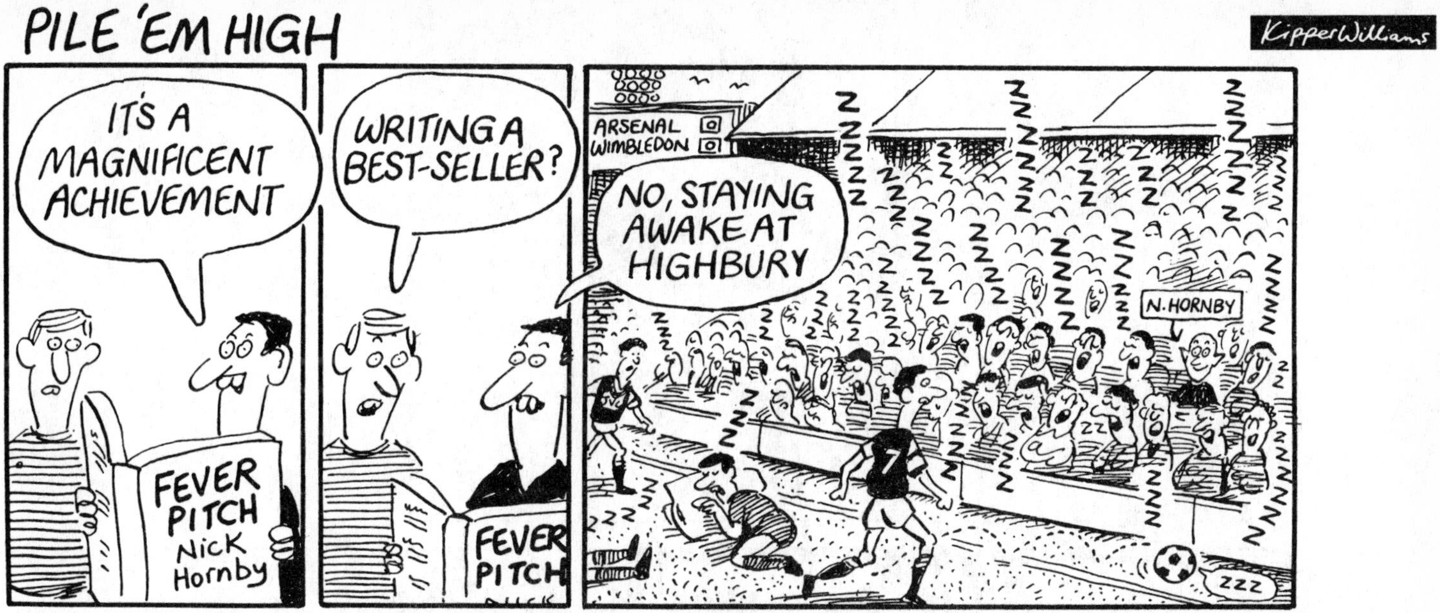
PILE 'EM HIGH
KipperWilliams
IT'S A MAGNIFICENT ACHIEVEMENT
FEVER PITCH
Nick Hornby
WRITING A BEST-SELLER?
FEVER PITCH
ARSENAL 0
WIMBLEDON 0
NO, STAYING AWAKE AT HIGHBURY
N. HORNBY
ZZZ

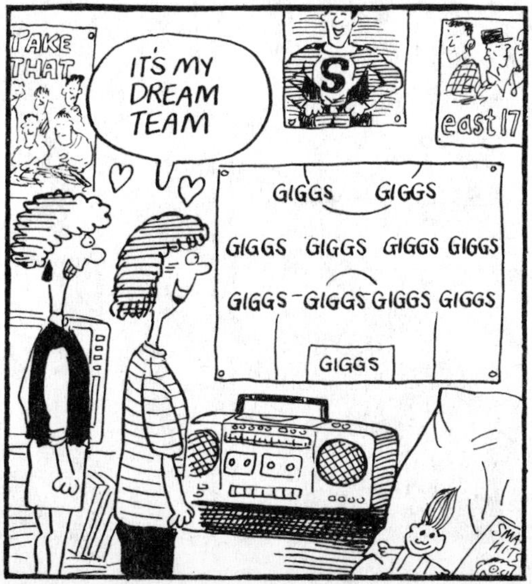
TAKE THAT
IT'S MY DREAM TEAM
east 17
GIGGS GIGGS
GIGGS GIGGS GIGGS GIGGS
GIGGS GIGGS GIGGS GIGGS
GIGGS

KipperWilliams

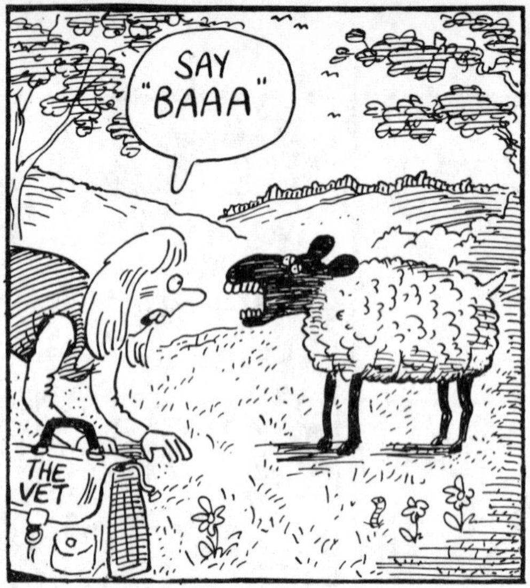
SAY "BAAA"
THE VET

PILE 'EM HIGH

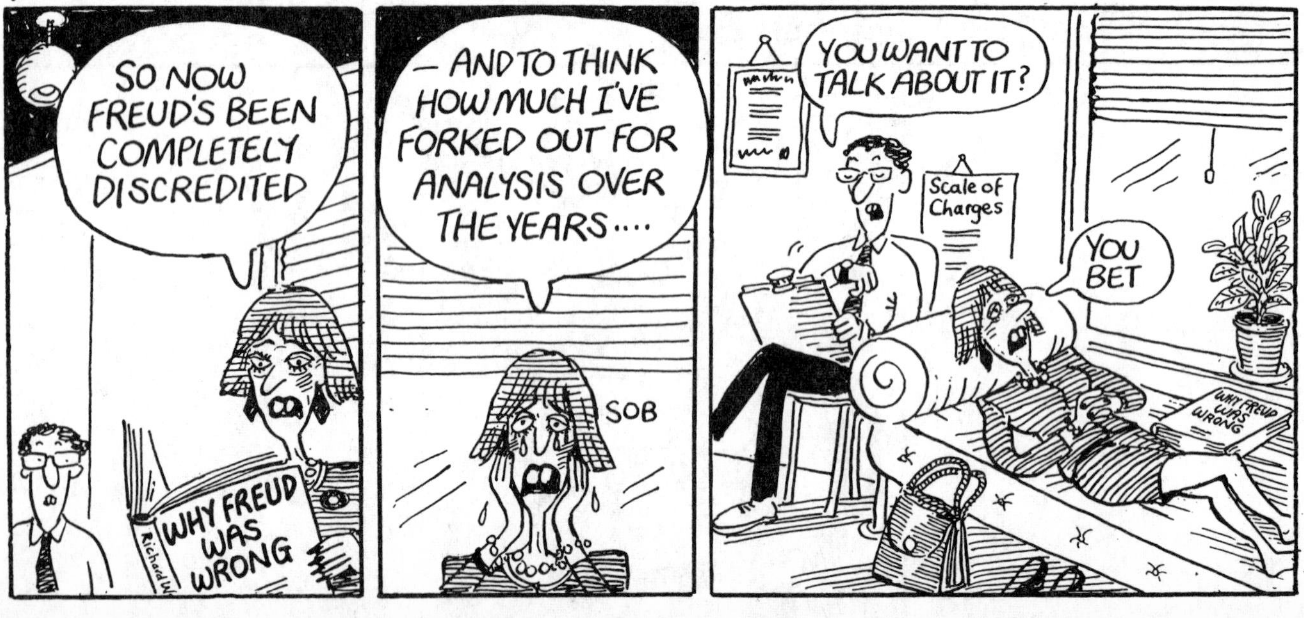
SO NOW FREUD'S BEEN COMPLETELY DISCREDITED
WHY FREUD WAS WRONG
– AND TO THINK HOW MUCH I'VE FORKED OUT FOR ANALYSIS OVER THE YEARS....
SOB
YOU WANT TO TALK ABOUT IT?
Scale of Charges
YOU BET
WHY FREUD WAS WRONG

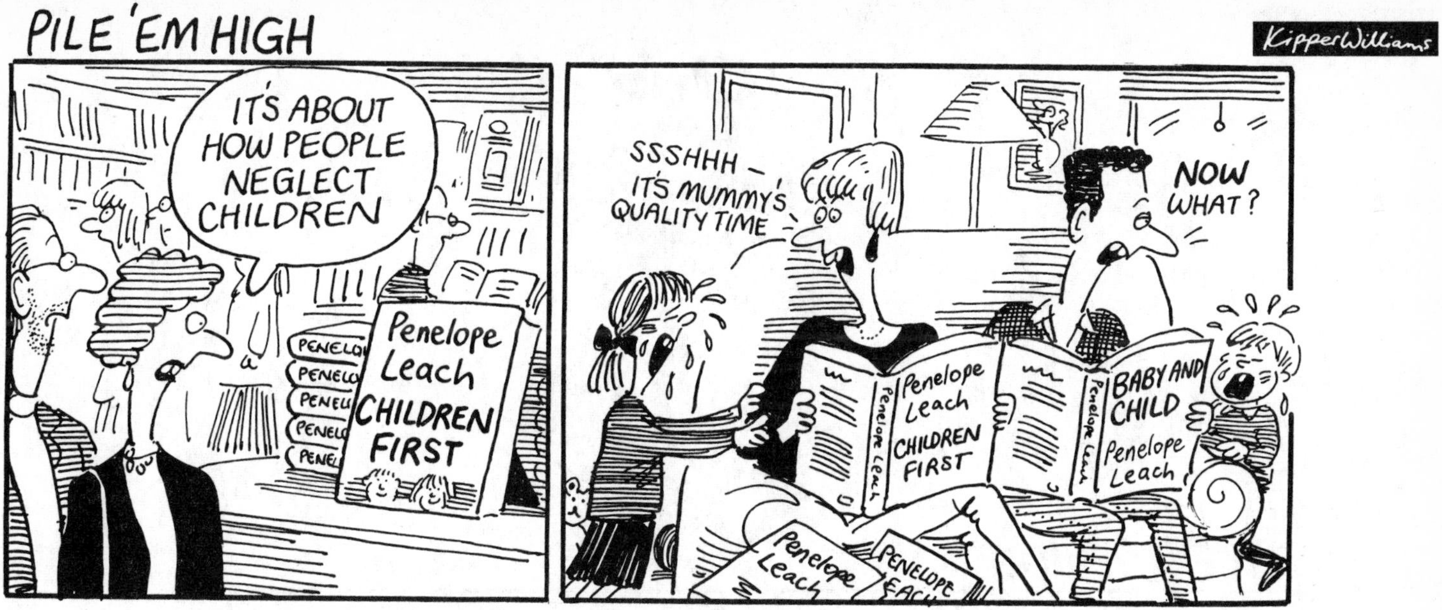
PILE 'EM HIGH
KipperWilliams
IT'S ABOUT HOW PEOPLE NEGLECT CHILDREN
Penelope Leach CHILDREN FIRST
SSSHHH – IT'S MUMMY'S QUALITY TIME
NOW WHAT?
Penelope Leach CHILDREN FIRST
BABY AND CHILD Penelope Leach
Penelope Leach

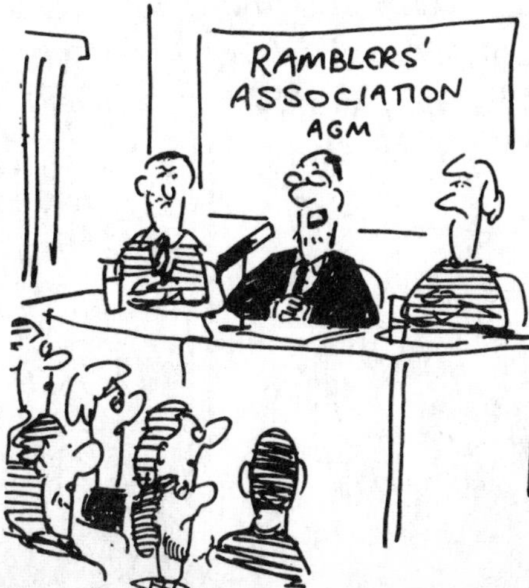
RAMBLERS' ASSOCIATION AGM

'But to get back to my main point.'

Club
Mad

PILE 'EM HIGH

...AND SO HAVING BEEN INVOLVED IN THIS APPALLING SEXUAL AND POLITICAL SCANDAL, I HAVE DECIDED TO RESIGN IN ORDER TO SPEND MORE TIME WITH MY FAMILY.
MP
WHERE'S DADDY?
IN THE STUDY WRITING HIS BLOCKBUSTER
TAP TAP TAP
TAP
TAP TAP
DO NOT DISTURB

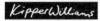

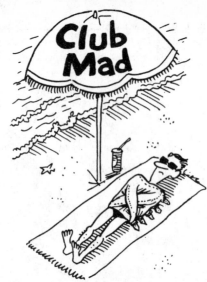

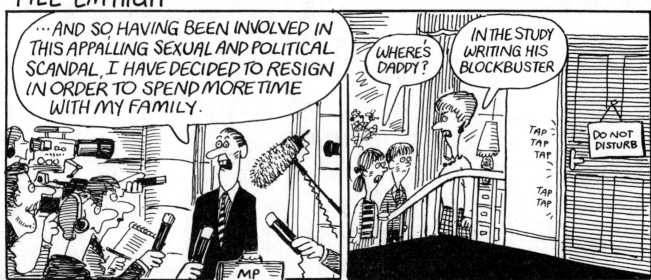

PILE 'EM HIGH

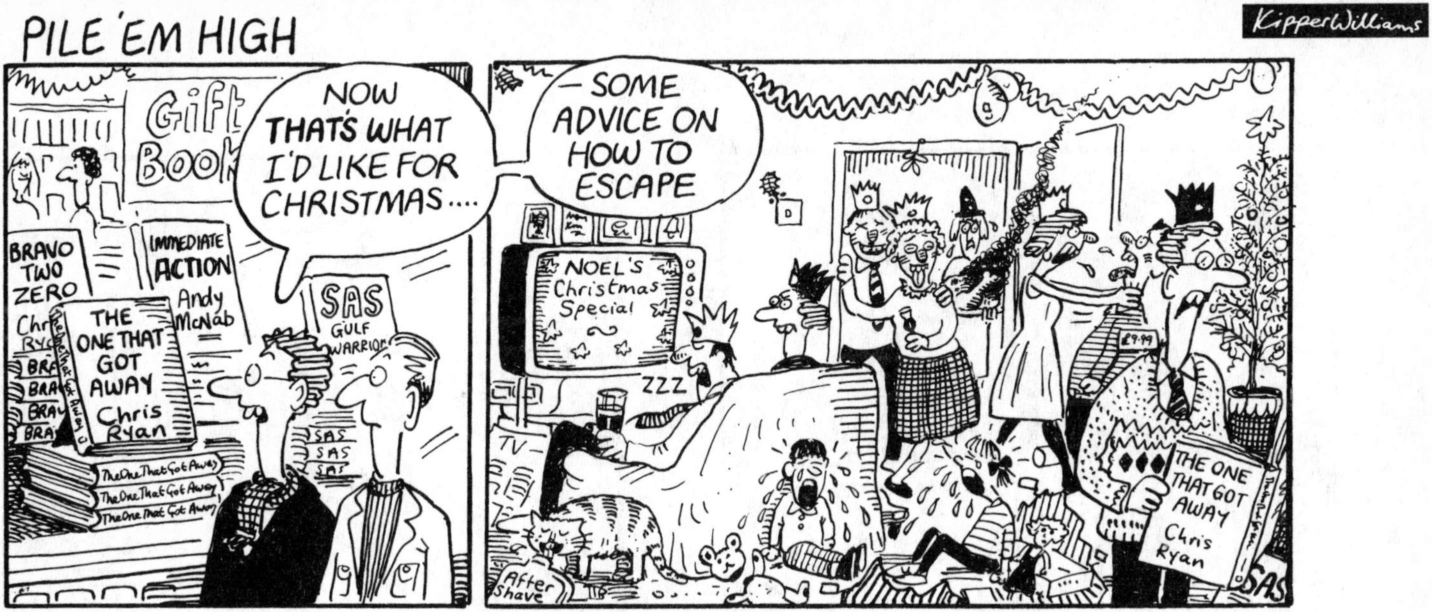
Kipper Williams
Gift
Book
BRAVO TWO ZERO
IMMEDIATE ACTION
Andy McNab
THE ONE THAT GOT AWAY
Chris Ryan
SAS
GULF WARRIOR
NOW THAT'S WHAT I'D LIKE FOR CHRISTMAS....
— SOME ADVICE ON HOW TO ESCAPE
NOEL'S Christmas Special
ZZZ
TV
After Shave
£9.99
THE ONE THAT GOT AWAY
Chris Ryan
SAS

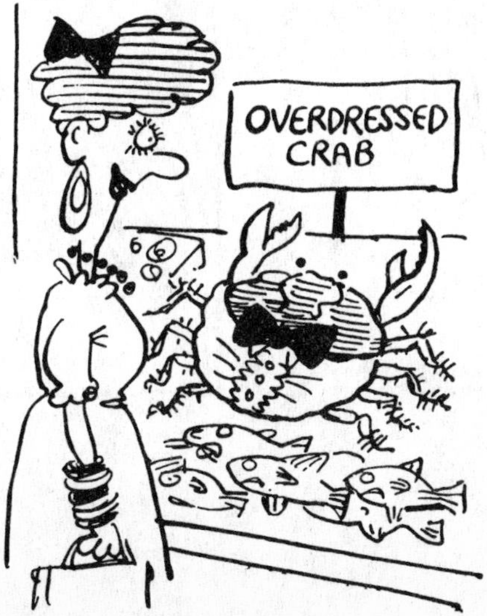
OVERDRESSED CRAB

KipperWilliams

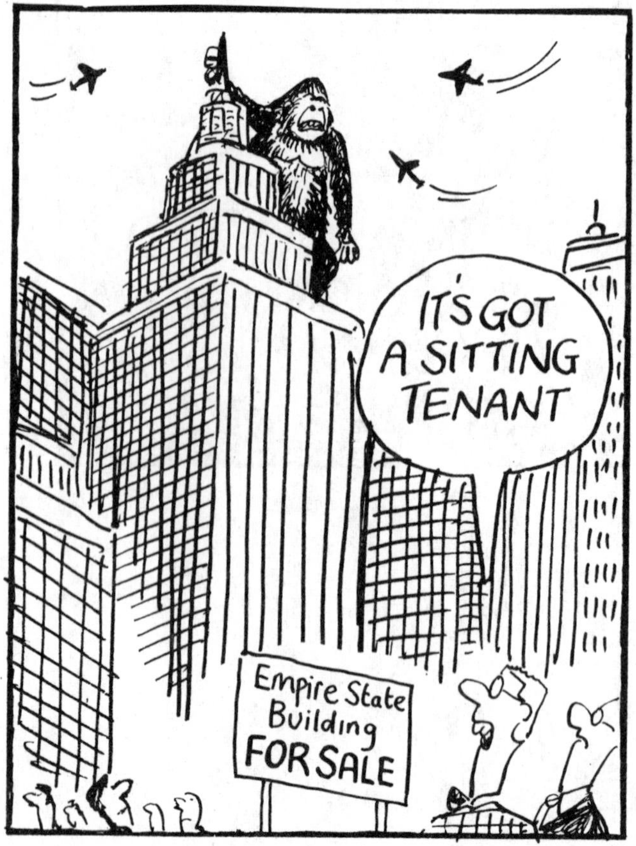
IT'S GOT A SITTING TENANT
Empire State Building FOR SALE

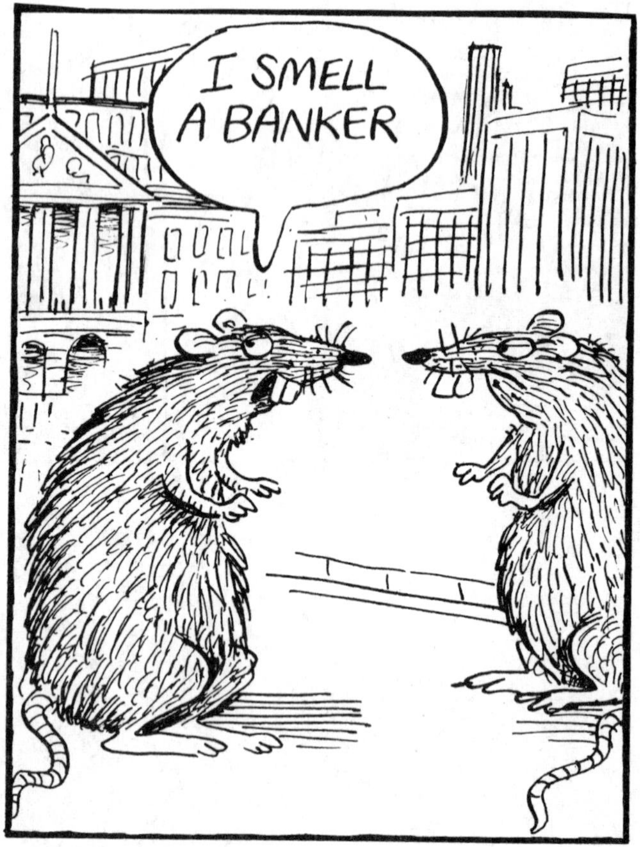
I SMELL A BANKER

KipperWilliams

Vampire's Arms
VLADS
VLASSES

GHENTS

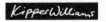

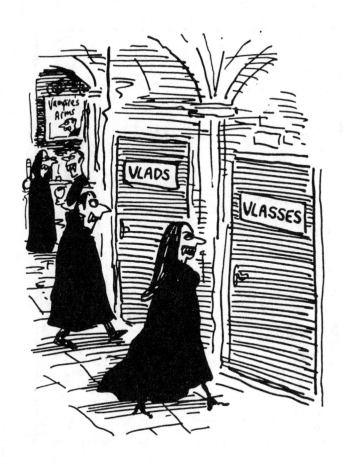

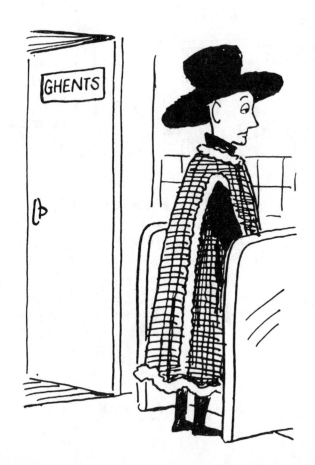

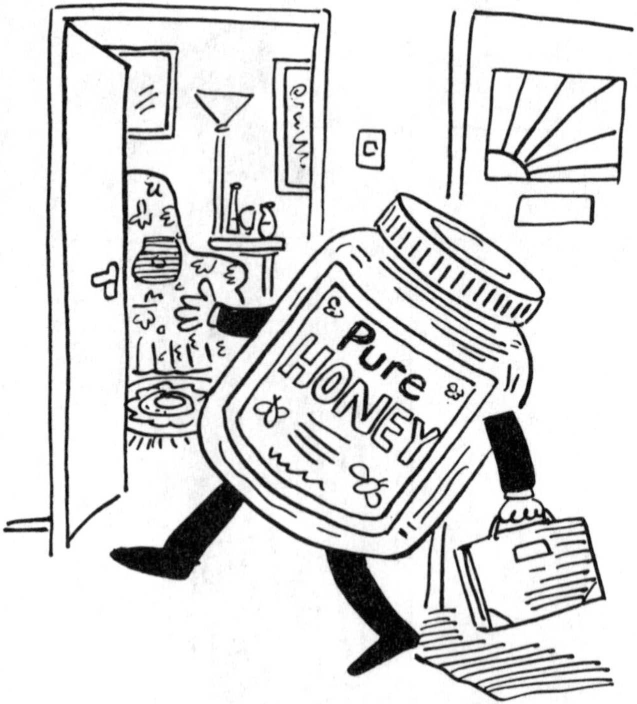
Pure
HONEY

'Hi, home, I'm honey!'

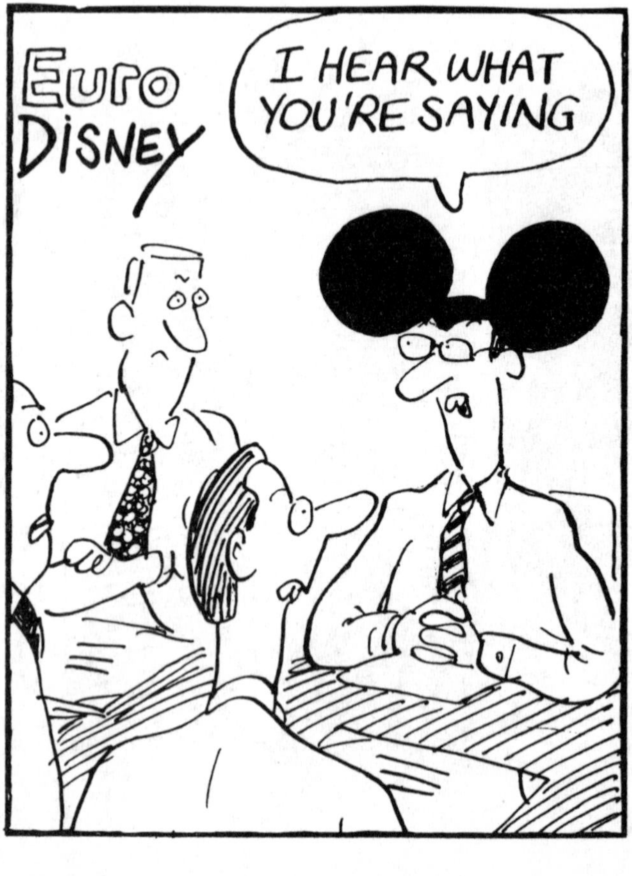
Euro
DISNEY
I HEAR WHAT YOU'RE SAYING

Eurocats

KipperWilliams

THEY WANT REVENGE.
Royal Visit to GERMANY
FREI RANGE EGGS
FOR 1945?
NO, 1966.
NOBBY STILES
NOBBY STILES
NOBBY STILES...
ÜBER ALLES

Menu
Menu

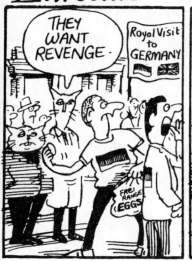

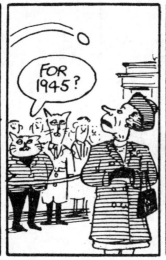

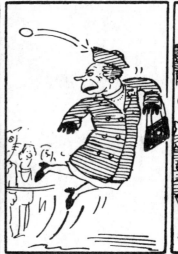

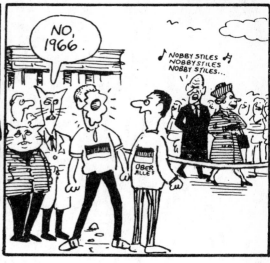

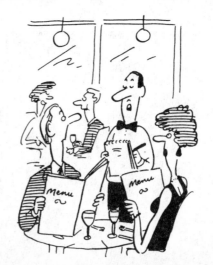

'How mad would you like your beef sir?'

KipperWilliams

chug chug
LONDON TO FOLKESTONE

Eurocats

THIS IS YOUR DRIVER SPEAKING. THERE'S BAD NEWS AND GOOD NEWS.
STAY WITH YOUR VEHICLE
EURO TUNNEL
WHAT'S THE BAD NEWS ?
THE TRAIN'S ON FIRE
EURO TUNNEL
WHAT'S THE GOOD NEWS ?
THE TUNNEL'S SPRUNG A LEAK !

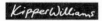

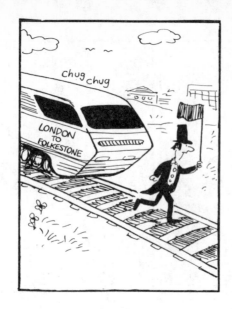

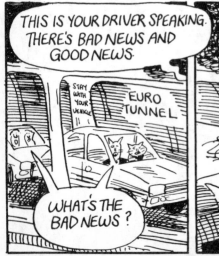

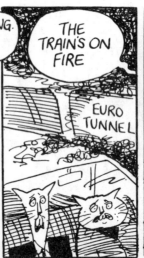

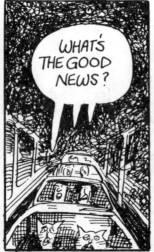

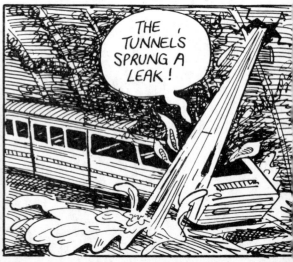

Eurocats

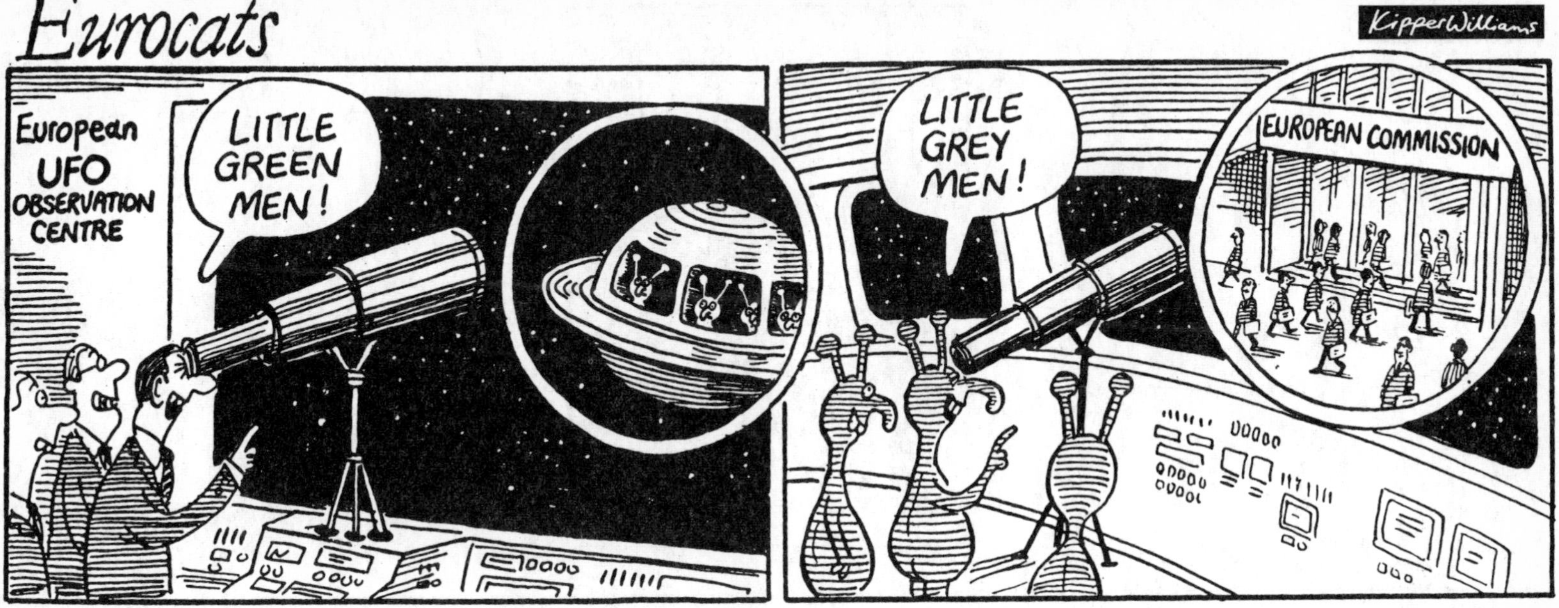
KipperWilliams
European UFO OBSERVATION CENTRE
LITTLE GREEN MEN!
LITTLE GREY MEN!
EUROPEAN COMMISSION

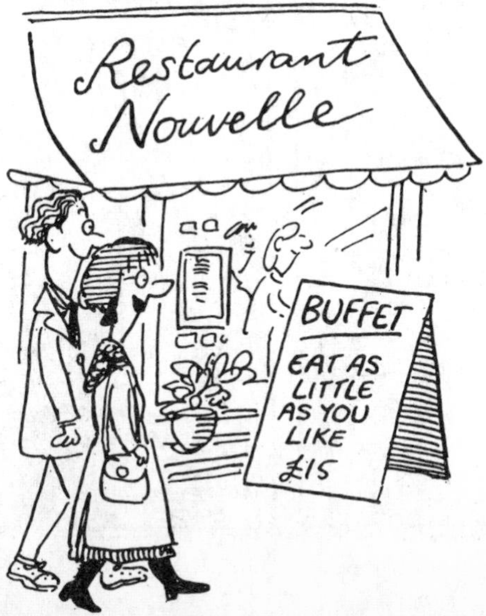
Restaurant Nouvelle
BUFFET
EAT AS LITTLE AS YOU LIKE £15

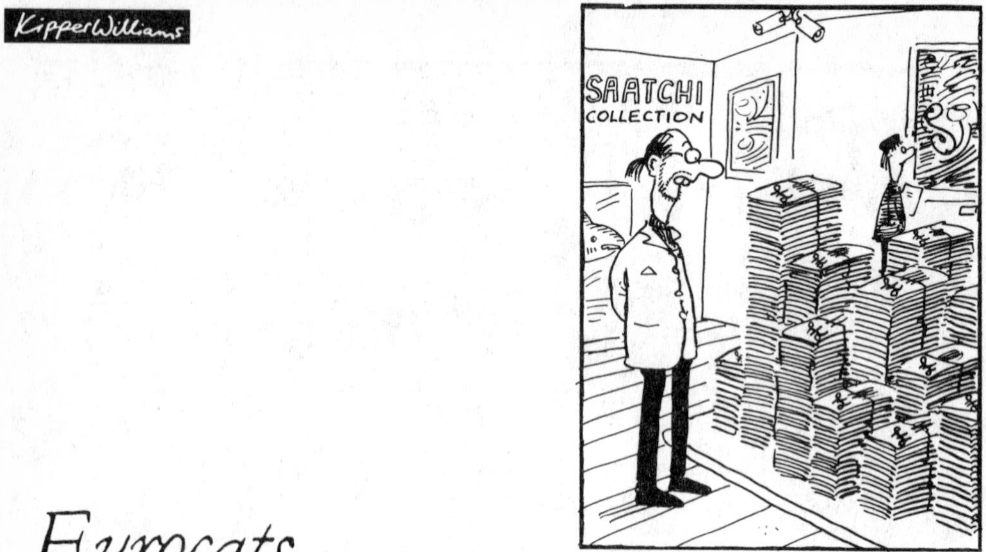
KipperWilliams
SAATCHI
COLLECTION

Eurocats

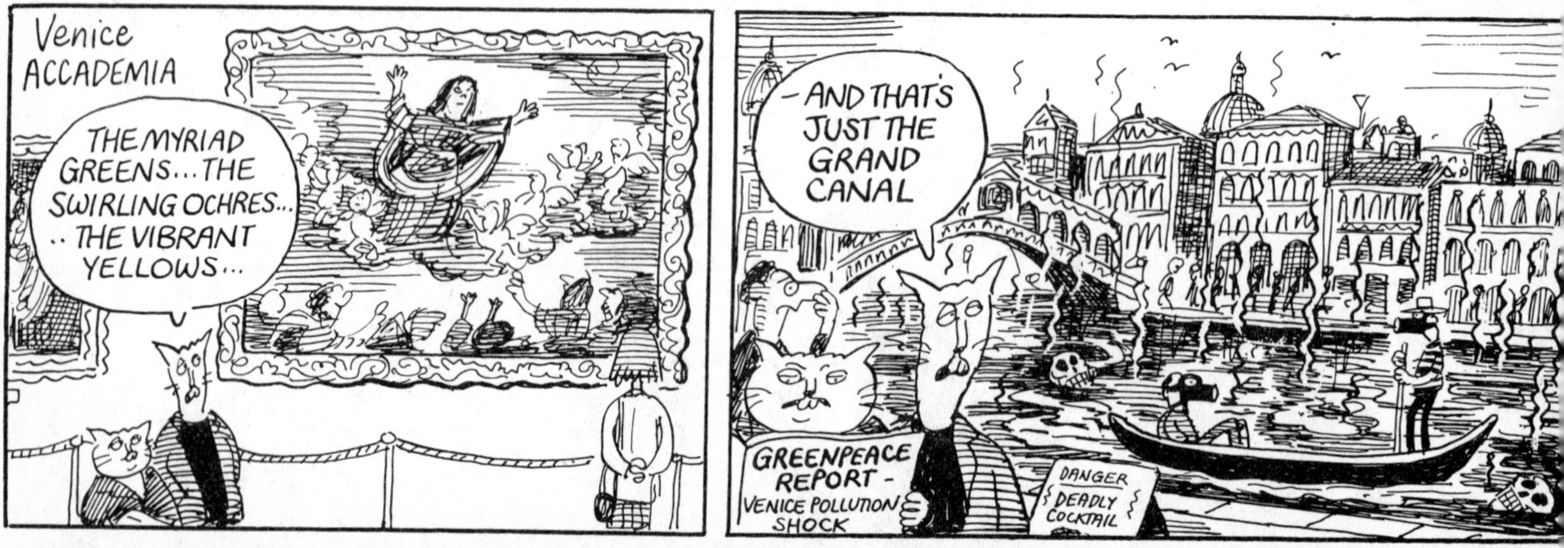
Venice
ACCADEMIA
THE MYRIAD GREENS... THE SWIRLING OCHRES... .. THE VIBRANT YELLOWS...
-AND THAT'S JUST THE GRAND CANAL
GREENPEACE REPORT -
VENICE POLLUTION SHOCK
DANGER
DEADLY COCKTAIL

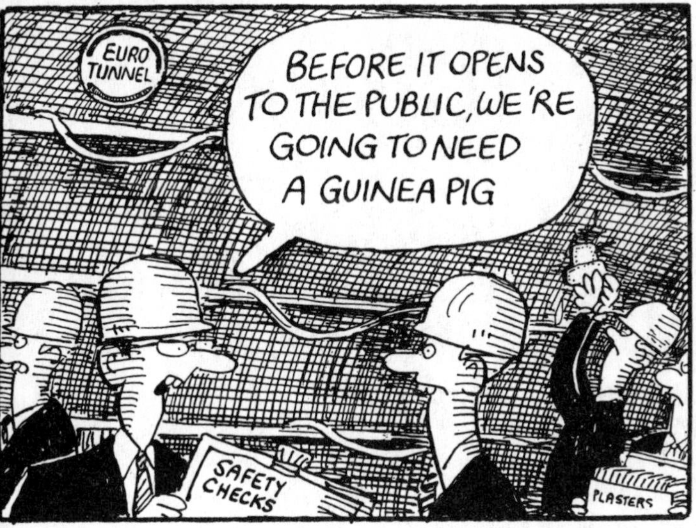
EURO TUNNEL
BEFORE IT OPENS TO THE PUBLIC, WE'RE GOING TO NEED A GUINEA PIG
SAFETY CHECKS
PLASTERS

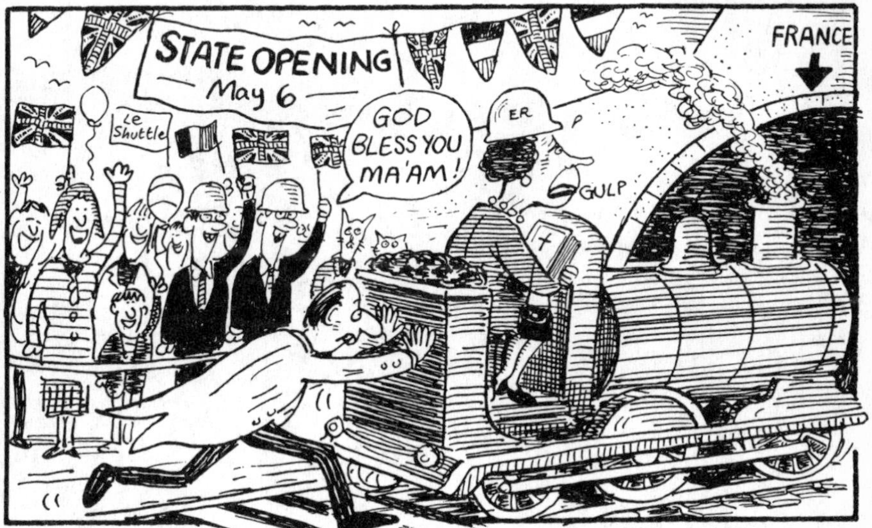
STATE OPENING
May 6
FRANCE
Le Shuttle
GOD BLESS YOU MA'AM!
ER
GULP

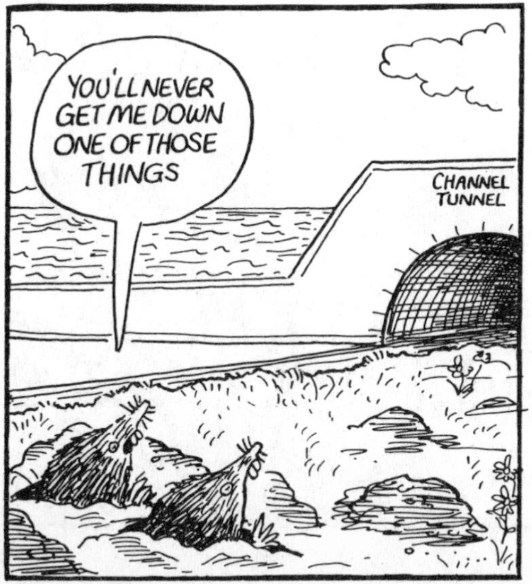
YOU'LL NEVER GET ME DOWN ONE OF THOSE THINGS
CHANNEL TUNNEL

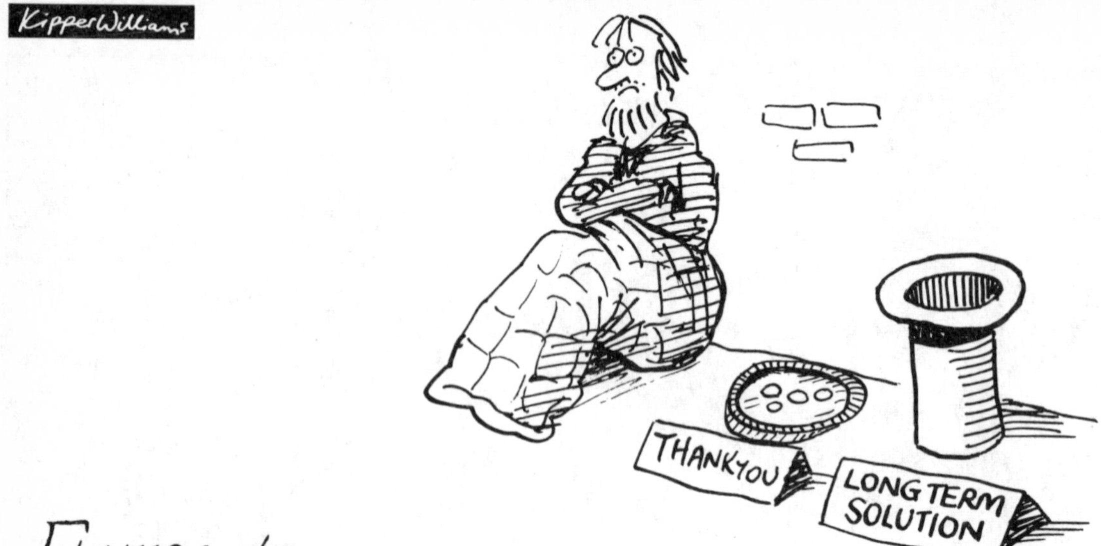
KipperWilliams
THANKYOU
LONG TERM SOLUTION

Eurocats

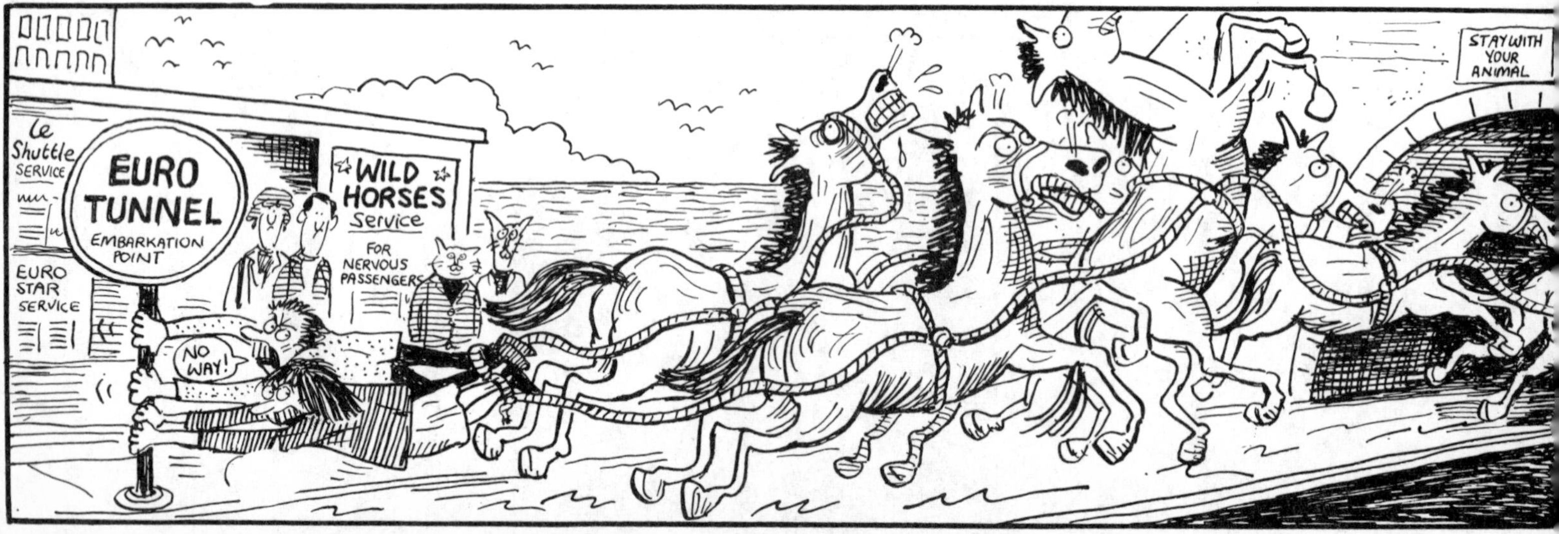
le Shuttle SERVICE
EURO TUNNEL
EMBARKATION POINT
EURO STAR SERVICE
WILD HORSES Service
FOR NERVOUS PASSENGERS
NO WAY!
STAY WITH YOUR ANIMAL

Eurocats

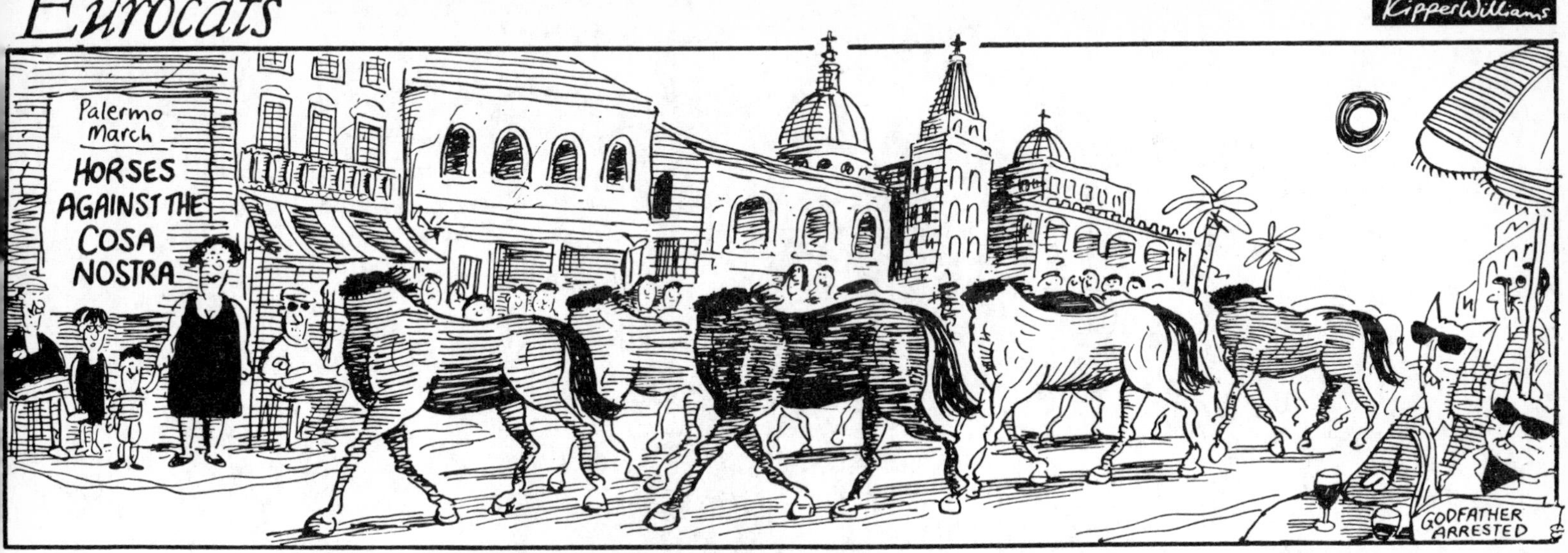
KipperWilliams
Palermo March
HORSES AGAINST THE COSA NOSTRA
GODFATHER ARRESTED

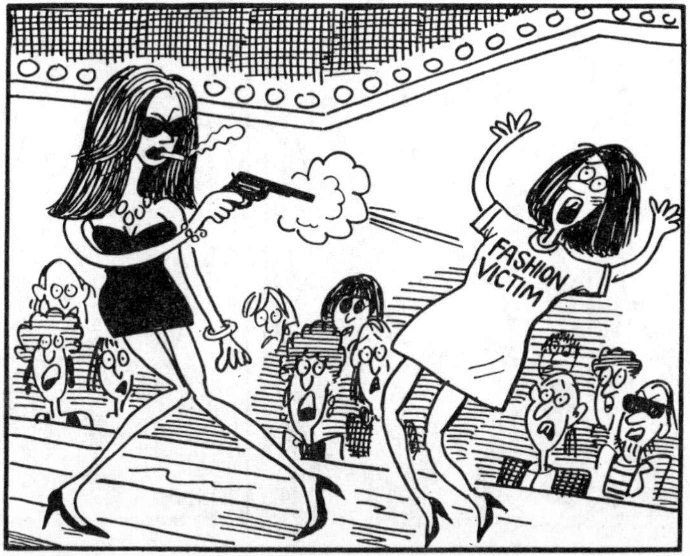
FASHION VICTIM

KipperWilliams

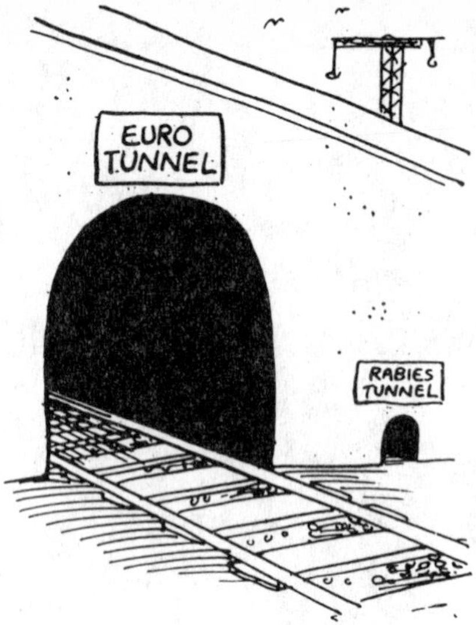
EURO TUNNEL
RABIES TUNNEL

Eurocats

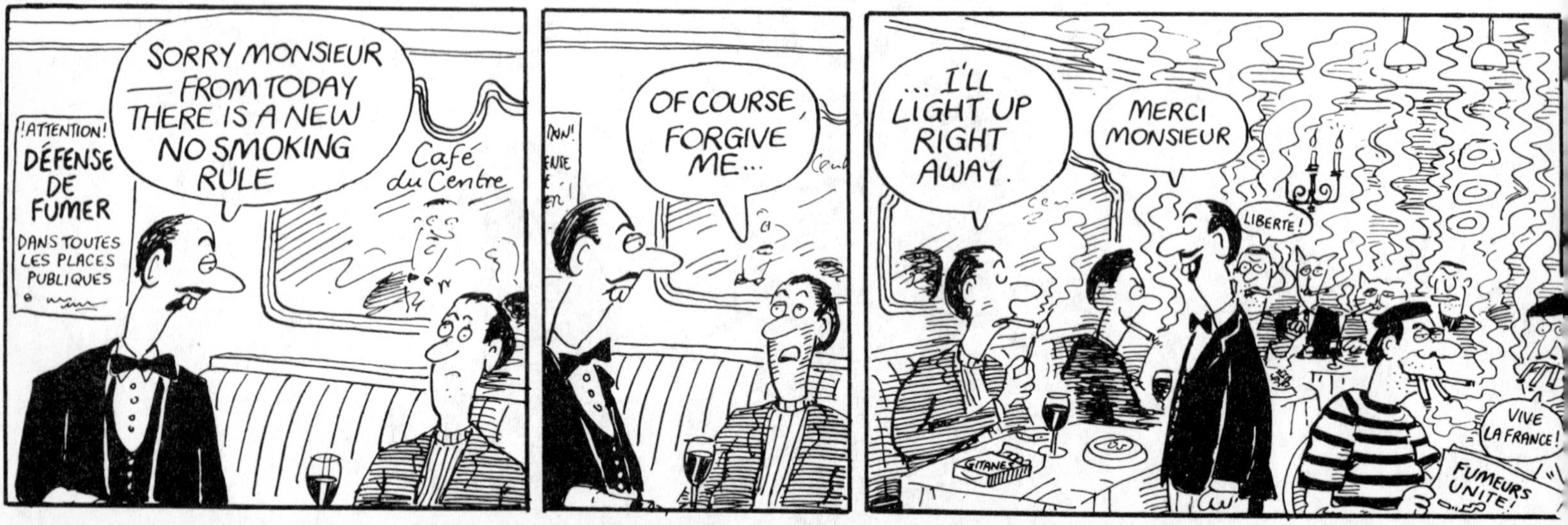
!ATTENTION! DÉFENSE DE FUMER DANS TOUTES LES PLACES PUBLIQUES
SORRY MONSIEUR — FROM TODAY THERE IS A NEW NO SMOKING RULE
Café du Centre
OF COURSE, FORGIVE ME...
... I'LL LIGHT UP RIGHT AWAY.
MERCI MONSIEUR
LIBERTÉ!
GITANES
VIVE LA FRANCE!
FUMEURS UNITÉ!

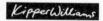

Eurocats

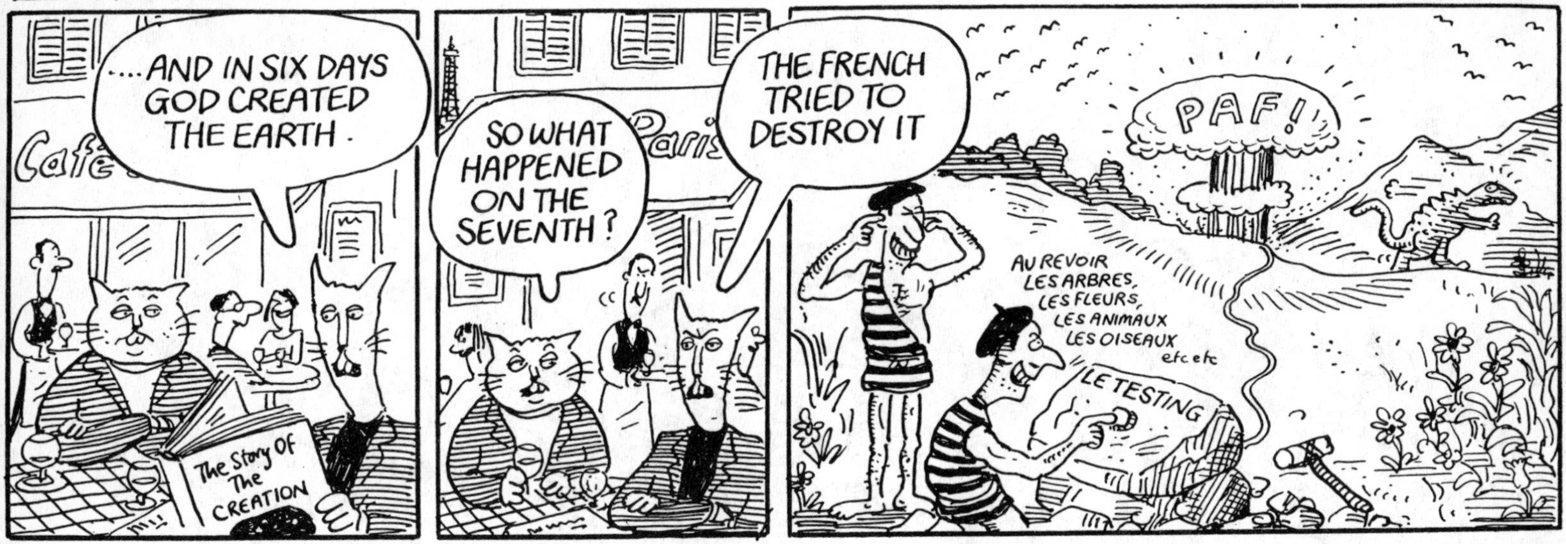
Kipper Williams
Café
....AND IN SIX DAYS GOD CREATED THE EARTH.
The Story Of The CREATION
Paris
SO WHAT HAPPENED ON THE SEVENTH ?
THE FRENCH TRIED TO DESTROY IT
PAF!
AU REVOIR LES ARBRES, LES FLEURS, LES ANIMAUX LES OISEAUX etc etc
LE TESTING

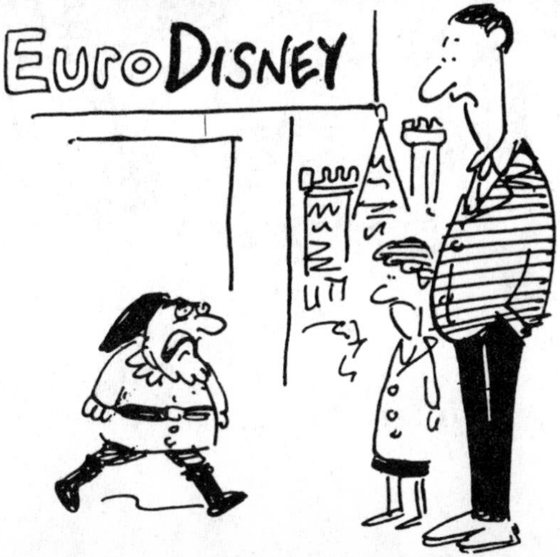
EURO DISNEY

'They sacked me for being Grumpy.'

'I ordered a tuna bap!'

'Not tonight, I've got a toothache.'

'He doesn't seem to be at his desk.'

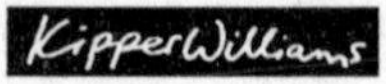
KipperWilliams

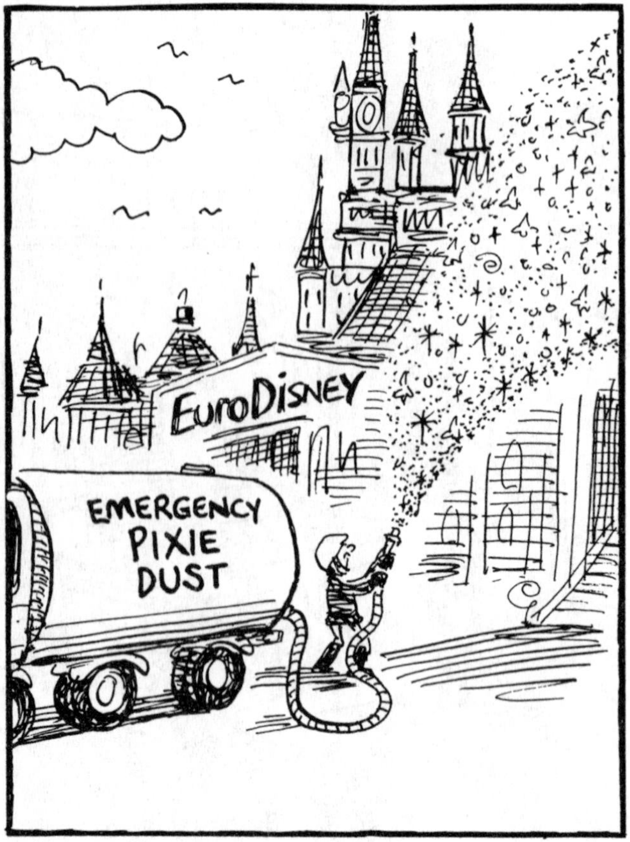
EuroDisney
EMERGENCY PIXIE DUST

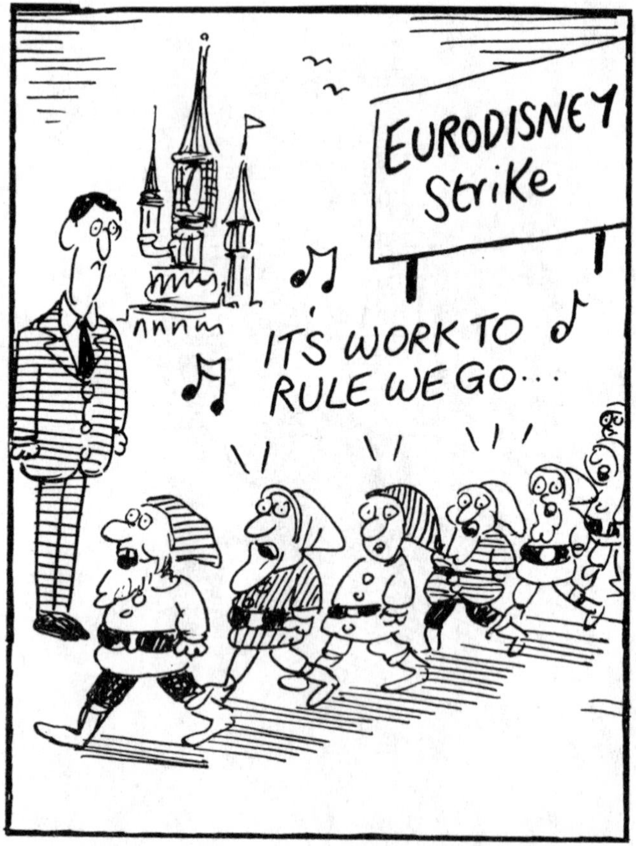
EURODISNEY Strike
IT'S WORK TO RULE WE GO...

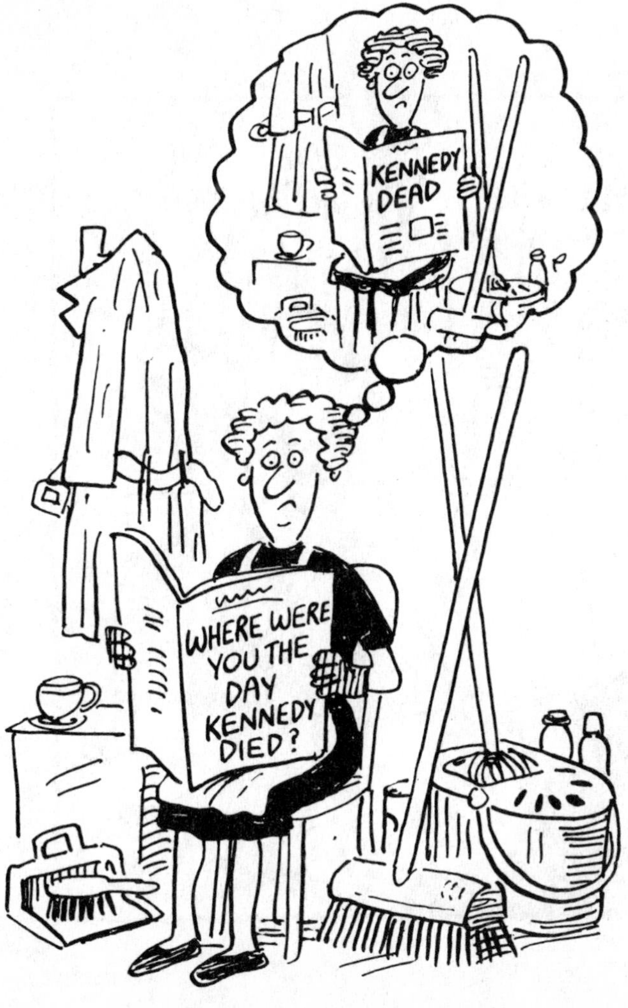
KENNEDY DEAD
WHERE WERE YOU THE DAY KENNEDY DIED?

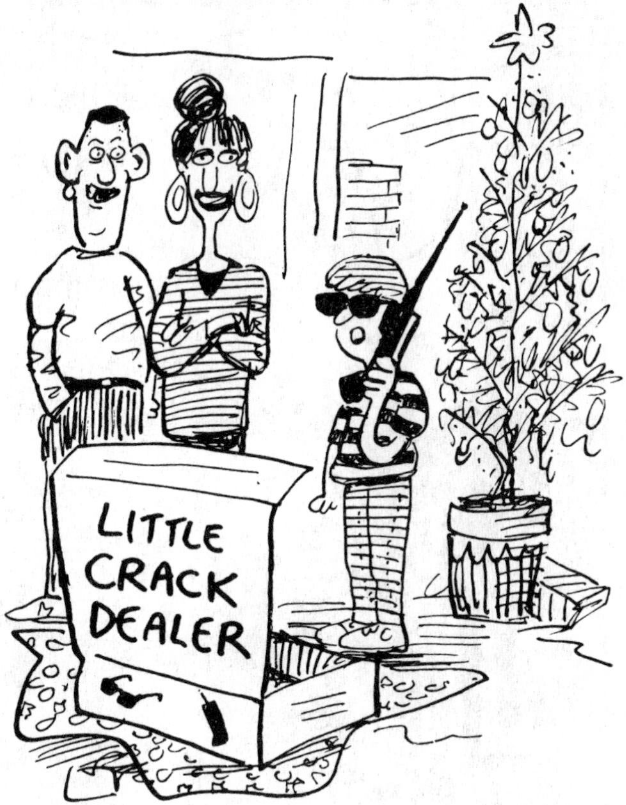
LITTLE CRACK DEALER

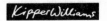

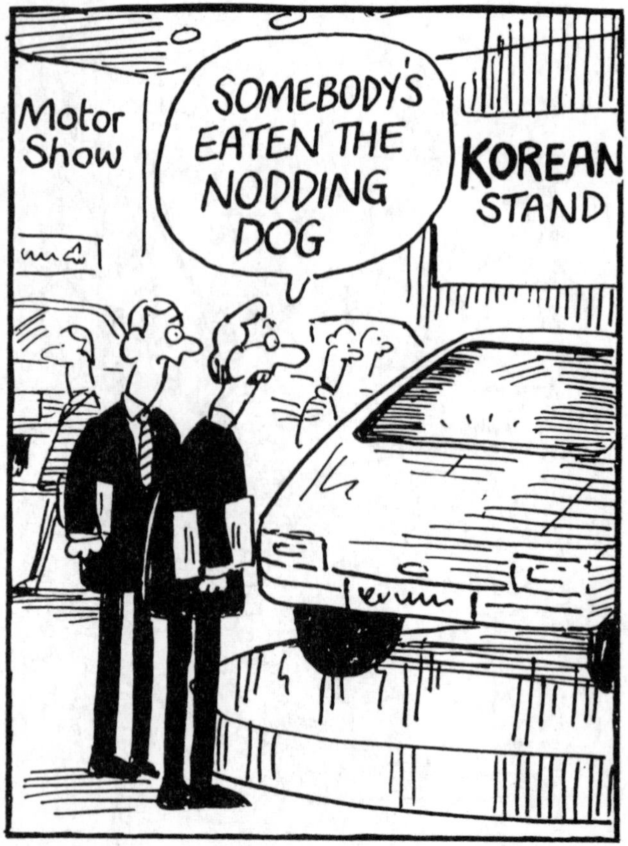
Motor Show
SOMEBODY'S EATEN THE NODDING DOG
KOREAN STAND

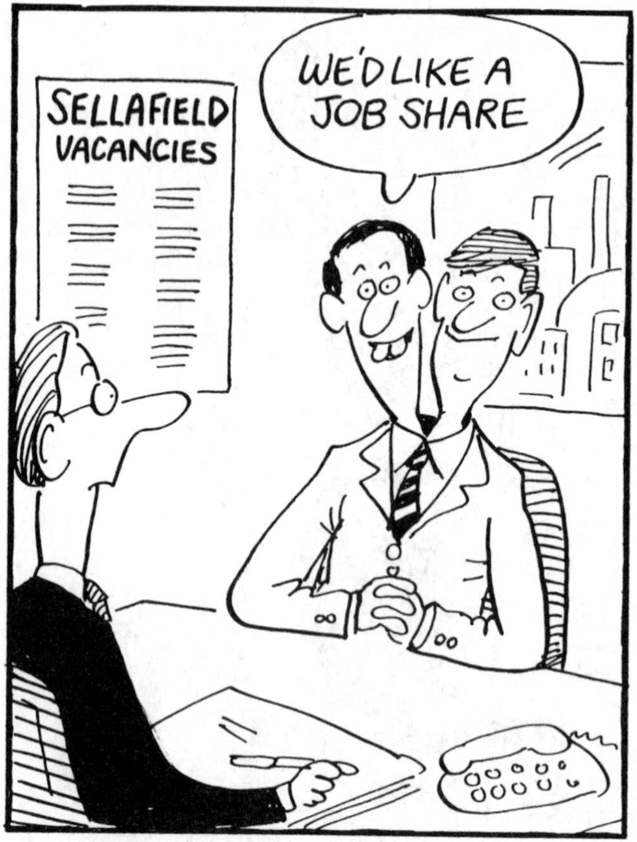
SELLAFIELD VACANCIES
WE'D LIKE A JOB SHARE

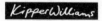

WHAT'S THE POINT OF GOLF?
?
ER...
?
A QUESTION OF SPORT

MATERNITY

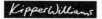

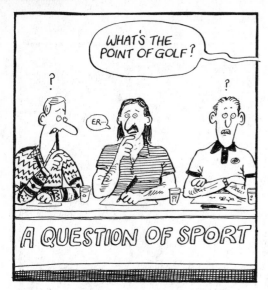

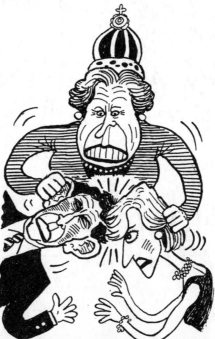

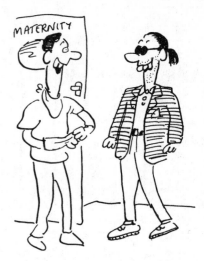

'Congratulations, it's a fashion accessory.'

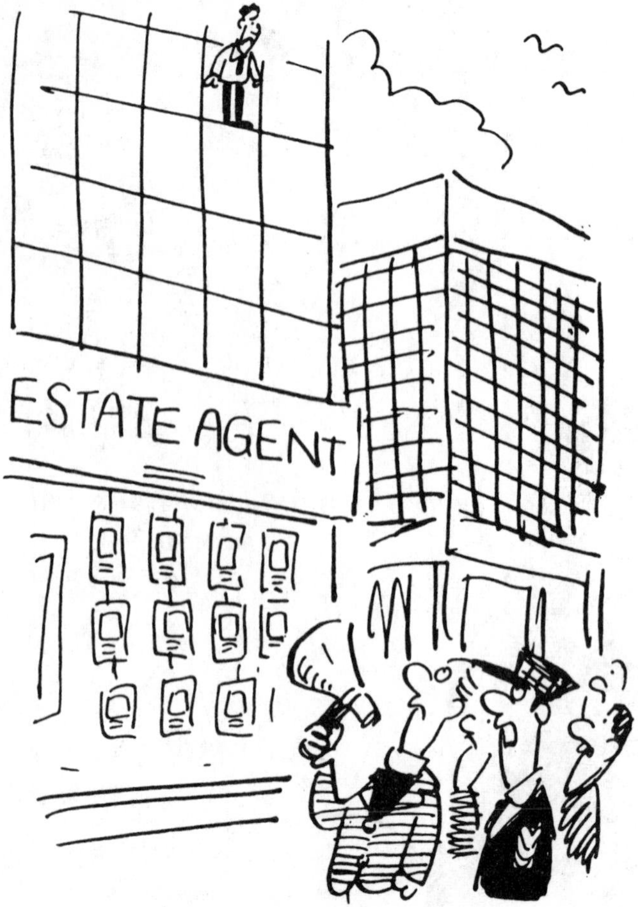
ESTATE AGENT

'Try making an offer.'

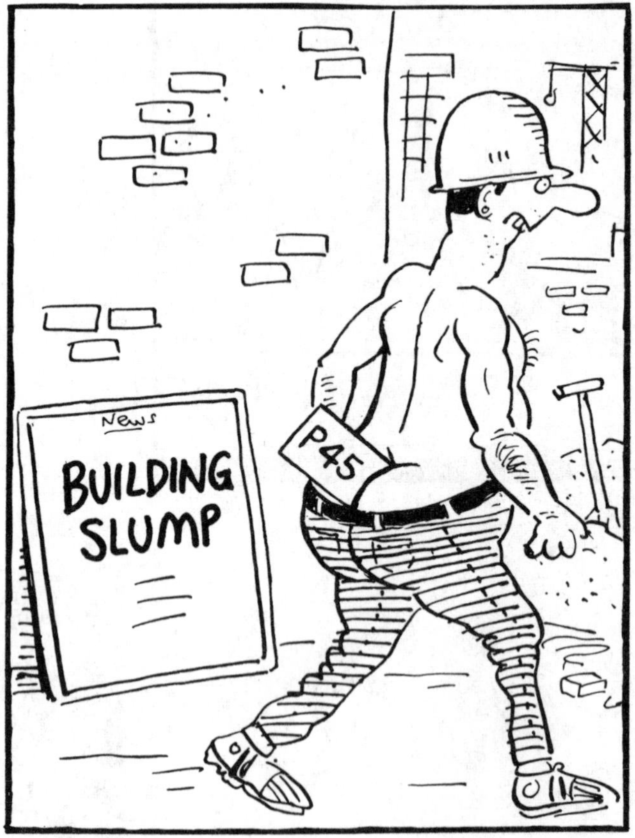
News
BUILDING SLUMP
P45

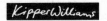